THE ART OF
RECRUITMENT

First published 2022 under the title *The Limitless Recruiter*
This edition first published 2022

Published under licence by Brown Dog Books and
The Self-Publishing Partnership Ltd, 10b Greenway Farm, Bath Rd,
Wick, nr. Bath BS30 5RL

www.selfpublishingpartnership.co.uk

ISBN printed book: 978-1-83952-433-2

ISBN e-book: 978-1-83952-434-9

Cover design by George Tunnah
Internal design by Andrew Easton

Printed and bound in the UK

This book is printed on FSC certified paper

Acknowledgements

First and foremost, a big thank you to all my family and friends who have assisted me throughout the past 39 years of my life, as well as all previous colleagues and professionals who have helped me in my career and business.

I'm also very grateful to Neil Sherreard – the man who took a chance on a recruiter with an idea and helped me launch Kingston Barnes into the company it is today. And to everyone at Kingston Barnes, past and present. You've all shaped our success and helped to build a passionate consultancy that is now on the map as a market leader. I'm so honoured to have shared so many memories and moments with you.

I'd like to thank Simon Toseland for his help with writing this book and for turning my many, many words, insights, stories and teachings into a legible, structured educational masterclass that will help empower future recruiters to become the next leaders of the industry.

I have been constantly inspired by Sir Richard Branson. His words and deeds gave me the courage and fortitude to take the leap to becoming an entrepreneur. He is a leader and visionary and I hope one day to emulate a fraction of his achievements. A great man who is changing the world we live in and whom I quote daily.

Another source of inspiration is the extreme adventurer and author, Ross Edgley. A man always breaking boundaries and teaching the true power and potential of resilience.

On a more personal note, my boys, Oliver and William. You

give me the fuel to keep driving the car forward – I am so proud of you both every minute of the day.

Mum and Dad. You taught me the value of hard work, humility, to never give up and always be a man of principle. I wish we had had more time together, but I am grateful for what we did have. You are always in my thoughts, and I miss you both every day.

Finally, Mrs. K. You inspire me to be all I can be, challenge me and push me to my potential, and I wouldn't be the man I am today without you.

THE ART OF
RECRUITMENT

HOW TO
BECOME A
LIMITLESS
RECRUITER

BROWN
DOG
BOOKS

"The essential guide to becoming an industry-leading recruiter"

Azmat Mohammed
Director-General of The British Institute of Recruiters

Table of Contents

PART ONE: THE RECRUITMENT INDUSTRY

Prologue: Learning The Hard Way

'Do not be embarrassed by your failures, learn from them and start again.' – Sir Richard Branson

The first temporary role I ever filled was handed to me on a plate. A site manager in a permanent position wanted to go freelance with the same company, as it would be financially more lucrative for him. His best friend worked on a temporary contract and was regularly showcasing his pay slip and boasting about his take-home pay. Because the site manager was one of the best around, and not easy to replace, the company felt they had no option but to go along with his wishes and so I placed him on a temporary contract with them. I negotiated a £5 per hour margin on a 50 hours per week arrangement. I was making the agency £250 per week. I patted myself on the back. Only 20 years old and it was looking like the world could be my oyster after all.

When this site manager then turned around and gave me my first vacancy to fill, I was made up. How easy was this recruitment business? It was a low-level position – a labouring job on a building site near Weston-super-Mare – and he wanted someone to start on Monday. It was Friday, so I got straight onto it. I found a suitable candidate for the job and gave him the details.

'It's a labouring position – you'll basically be moving materials from one place to another, tidying up, keeping the site clean – free from waste and rubbish – that sort of thing,' I told him over the phone.

'Yeah, sounds good to me, that's what I've been doing for the last six months,' he said.

'Can you start on Monday?' I asked.

'Sure, no problem.'

I gave him the address, agreed the rate of pay. Job done. They had needed a labourer – the most basic job in the world – what could go wrong? I'd made my second placement and I was elated.

First thing on Monday morning, the office phone rang. They asked for me. It was the site manager. What could he want? To give me another job? To say how much he appreciated the service I was giving him? I grinned at the experienced consultant sitting next to me.

'James. Where's his hard hat and high vis?'

'Excuse me? What do you mean?'

'Where's his hard hat and hi vis jacket? He's turned up without them and we can't let him work on site until he's got them.'

The consultant next to me was smirking. I had to grab a hard hat and hi vis jacket and borrow his Ford Focus – my bora bora green Citroën Xsara was in the garage – and get down to the site sharpish. My candidate was wasting the company's time and losing me credibility. Back then we didn't have satnav and the site was in the middle of nowhere, of course. I had to keep stopping to check the route finder I had printed out, next to me on the passenger seat. So, there I was, a bright spark of a 20-year-old, rocking up one and a half hours after my temp was meant to have started his job but couldn't, because he hadn't turned up with the right equipment. Eventually I found the site, gave the man the hard hat and jacket, smoothed things over with the client and left.

As I headed back to the office in Bristol, I reflected on what had happened. Now, most labourers have their own personal protective equipment (PPE) – boots and a hard hat are the minimum requirements for a labouring job – but I hadn't checked. I hadn't checked with the company that he'd need them and I hadn't checked with the candidate that he had them. Instead, I'd had to waste half a day driving down to a site to deliver some basic equipment. That was the first important lesson I learned about recruitment – *make sure you take a detailed job spec*. I hadn't asked the question, instead I had just assumed, and assumptions – as the saying goes – had made a massive ass out of me.

That's recruitment, though. If you think you've got it nailed then you're definitely preparing to fail. There is always something new to learn, always a better way to do something you may have done a thousand times already. Every candidate, every job, every client and every company is different, and if you don't continue to listen and learn – and sometimes follow your gut – then you'll soon get pulled up.

That's why I wrote this book.

I've achieved a lot in my twenty years in recruitment, from placing over a thousand candidates to building a multi-million-pound, multi-award-winning recruitment agency. There are major differences between a bad recruiter and a good recruiter, but the gaps between an average recruiter and the best recruiters are a little harder for some to spot. Having been in the heart of the recruitment industry for nearly two decades, working with the best recruiters in the sector, I was intrigued about what makes an elite recruiter – a Limitless Recruiter. So I picked it all apart, including myself, to find out what the ingredients are and what the recipe is that makes a recruiter exceptional. What is it in their DNA that makes the best recruiters?

As I explain later in this book, a Limitless Recruiter has the perfect combination of a growth mindset and a tremendous work ethic. They excel in their knowledge of the industry and in building relationships with clients and candidates. They consistently improve their performance through strategic planning and multiple goal-setting. Because of their application and time-management, the only limit to their success is the scope of their ambition.

In these pages are foolproof methods, watertight processes, tried and tested tips and tricks which will turn you into an exceptional recruiter, whether you're just thinking about recruitment as a career, are starting out on your first job in the industry, or have been in the business for years and want to develop. Look upon me as your mentor. I've been there, done that and got the T-shirt in every size, shape and colour, and most importantly, I know how to excel at it. I'll guide you through all the different aspects you'll need to help you become a Limitless Recruiter – capable of an elite-level career performance. Welcome to the recruitment masterclass.

Hopefully, I'll also inspire and entertain you on the way with real-life experiences – the things I've learned from failure as well as success: recruitment is the best job in the world when it's going well – and all the tools you need to make sure every recruiting day is a great recruiting day are contained in these pages. Follow my advice and I guarantee you'll be a better consultant than you ever thought possible. Remember and believe this, there are no limits to what you can achieve with the right mindset and the right advice. Oh, and don't forget your hard hat.

James Kingston
December 2021

Chapter One: Knowing My Place

The first placement I ever made was Rob. He was my best friend at school, and I placed him with Claire – a lovely girl I'd grown up with. This was on New Year's Eve in 1996 and I was 14 years old. I just knew they'd be good together and so I strategically introduced them to each other at the right time, said a few nice things and watched my great plan unfold before my eyes. Now, 25 years later, they're still together – happily married, with two adorable children. Not all my matches have worked out as well.

I was born and raised in Bristol and have lived here for all of my 39 years. My mother was a single parent who raised my little sister and me in Staple Hill, which was not one of the posher areas of Bristol. Back then, it was solidly working class. We didn't have much money – you could have classed us as poor – but we were a happy, close-knit family.

Four things about me have been constant. One – I was always a chatterbox who used to get told off at school for talking too much. Two, I have always loved sport. I would play anything – and was pretty good at everything I took up. Three, I was always very competitive – no matter what I did, I had to be the best at it and I believed I could be (and I still do). And four, most importantly, I never took 'no' for an answer. These four traits combined in my passion for football. From a young age, I quickly became a big Bristol City fan. I still follow the Robins, though the days of going to every match are long gone. I've got a young family now, so unless I'm taking a client to a match, my opportunities are limited.

From the age of 14, though, when I used to go and watch City, I had a group of six friends who quite often couldn't afford it or didn't want to go, and I considered it a challenge to see how many of them I could round up for each game. I would pick up the phone and spend between five and twenty minutes diligently persuading each of them to go to the match. I used to get a real thrill from every successful call and I guess that's one of the first instances in my life where I showed a talent for sales – especially given how the Robins were doing back then.

I have no idea where this knack comes from. My father worked in a job he didn't love at Rolls Royce for nearly 50 years just to put food on the table. He was of the generation where you went to work to provide for your family. End of. He was 16 when he started work there and 64 when he left. My mother didn't work – she struggled with poor mental health from an early age and was diagnosed with bipolar disorder in her thirties.

When my parents separated, I went to live with Mum, as did my younger sister. Mum was on benefits. We weren't poverty stricken, but I noticed differences. At school all my friends would be going on lovely holidays, spending their weekends doing various interesting activities, regularly going out to nice restaurants and getting great presents for their birthdays and at Christmas. I had to buy clothes with any money I was given. The best thing I ever ate before I was 24 years old was on my annual birthday treat to the Harvester. We'd holiday occasionally, camping in Cornwall every few years. That for me was the norm. I promised myself that once I was able to, I would be in complete control of my own destiny and I would never be held back by a lack of money.

I was an average achiever at school – teachers said I had lots of ability and a lot of potential, but I always got distracted in class and wasn't motivated academically. I enjoyed going to school primarily to network and socialise, to talk to people – that's where the excitement was for me. I didn't get much out of school academically, except for subjects like History and Drama, where there was debate or acting involved.

One of the traits of the Limitless Recruiter – it's in their DNA – is an ability to interact with people. A lot of them are extroverts. I was often the loudest person in the room – the most talkative. I wanted to be in the conversation, in the know, liked by everyone and included in all the social circles. A popular person.

When I was studying A Levels, it wasn't that common to go to university – certainly no one in my family ever had – but I fancied my chances, and I knew what I wanted to do. I wanted to be a film director, as I had been obsessed with movies from an early age. My favourites were always those which focused on the underdog. Films like *Rocky, Star Wars, Good Will Hunting, Remember the Titans,* and my all-time go-to movie, *The Shawshank Redemption*. I studied English Language and History in sixth form, then went on to college to study Media and Communication, because I wanted to get into the movie industry. But then I met someone who put me off it completely. She was a successful television producer who had studied at my college. We got chatting – I'd chat with anyone, remember – and I told her about my ambitions. During our conversation she said,

'Film and TV is a great industry but it's all very Oxbridge and contact-led – it's about who you know, rather than what you know. Six months of the year you could be living the dream in a penthouse in London; the other six months – after working on a production – you could be back with your parents in the spare room, living on pot noodles.'

This really hit home. I'd already been accepted on a Film and Media degree course at the University of Plymouth. Everything was in place and I was ready to go. I could see the next three years of my life unfolding before me. But then I thought, *Do I really want to spend the rest of my life in an industry I might not be able to influence or succeed in*? Up until then I'd always been in an environment where I felt in control of my own success, but something didn't feel right in my gut and so I decided, *No, that's not for me*. People thought I was mad, but I went with my instincts. It was the best decision I ever made, career-wise.

From an early age I always worked hard at everything I did. I had a paper round which I did on roller-skates – I still, to this day, love to roller-skate. When I went to secondary school, I got a job putting up skittles in the local pub on Tuesday and Thursday evenings. I earned £15 for the whole night. At chucking-out time I'd roller-skate home and get back at about midnight. The first proper job I got was at the Harvester, ironically, when I was 15 – the scene of all my birthday treats. I had to pretend I was 16 to get the job and I worked behind the bar – not serving alcohol but bar food, clearing up and washing glasses.

In the sixth form I worked at Matalan at weekends and had my first call centre job with Orange – the mobile phone company – when I started college. I was working a 30-hour week at Orange, on the phone, while I was studying. It was inbound call centre work, largely dealing with queries and complaints from unhappy customers. I got average grades at A Level – enough to get me a place at Plymouth Uni. I found a new hobby at the gym and started body-building. I loved the routine, discipline and being able to do things not a lot of others could. I just wanted to stand out.

When I declined Uni I thought, *Shit, what am I going to do*? I was a 19-year-old working-class boy with no clear sense of direction anymore. I looked around and ended up working at the Child Support Agency as a case officer. My mum reckoned working in the Civil Service was the perfect job – she used to go on about it – so I thought, *Okay, I'll give it a go*. It wasn't a great working environment. It was a low-paid Civil Service job, and you could knock off early, so a lot of people were there for the work-life balance, rather than the actual work.

I hated being there – the work was slow and tedious. I was bored. The best thing was my colleagues, who I loved chatting with. I also used to enjoy tracking down the people who were avoiding paying child support because, for me, if you have a child you have to take that responsibility seriously. I soon found out there were plenty of absent parents who didn't want to pay, which meant ultimately the taxpayer had to subsidise them, and that really annoyed me. So, I had to head-hunt these people, which was the only part of the job I relished – at least it was a challenge.

After a year, I thought, *Do you know what? I'm never going to get anywhere with this. I'm never going to earn real money and have the life that I always dreamed of.* I've always been quite ambitious – I wanted to have all the finer things in life that I hadn't had as a child. More importantly, I'd always thought that if I had children, I'd want to give them a life where money wasn't an issue.

I wanted to have a life where I could do what I wanted to – whether that was buying a nice car, a house to be proud of, travelling around the world or making sure my children had the best education available.

When I was young, I'd wanted to go to Colston's School – a prestigious private school in Bristol – and I got as far as a half-scholarship, but my parents couldn't afford to contribute the rest, so sadly I missed out on that fantastic education and experience.

That's where my son, Oliver, goes now and it has been one of my proudest achievements to see him flourish from it.

I didn't want to be limited by not having money, so I sat there thinking, *What am I going to do*? I was still living at home with Mum, I'd got my first car, and I was 19 years old. Whilst I was still full-time at the CSA, I took a job with a local home improvement specialist, basically selling double glazing. It was telesales, two evenings a week. Each night I had to make X number of calls and have X number of conversations, and then book appointments for other salespeople to go and persuade potential customers to buy the products and services on offer.

THE ART OF RECRUITMENT

'The key to anything in sales is relationship-building.'
– James Kingston

I loved it. Within a week I was the best telesales agent and I was exceeding my targets. Remember, I was a chatterbox and highly competitive. The way I approached it was to view it as a challenge. I knew that to succeed, I needed to talk to as many people as possible, but in a way that was positive, rather than in the confrontational, pushy or aggressive manner of a lot of the other agents. I thought, if I can be nice and get them to have a chat, they'll open up and I'll have a higher chance of success. At the very least, I'll build up a relationship with them and they'll go away with a good impression of me and the company.

I looked at what I could control about the process. The obvious thing was to make more calls than the night before, speak to more people than before, and look for the best ways to get around the same objections that came up time after time – *'We don't really need new windows; I can't afford it; I'm busy; no thank you – goodbye'.* I turned it into a game and suddenly it became enjoyable.

The company had a template script, but within a week I'd thrown it out of the window and written my own. The key to anything in sales is relationship-building. You've got to be able to have a proper conversation with someone and get to know their needs. Not everyone is going to want what you've got to sell, but at some point they might.

Empathy was the key to it all, and something I always had with people. From being the only man in the house, then spending a year in an office full of women at the CSA, I had got to understand women a bit better than many of my male friends, and women are naturally much better communicators than men. I just had to understand where the client was coming from.

'Look,' I'd say, *'I know you've had sales calls from people you don't want to talk to. I'm offering you something for free which, if you are interested in, you can take up and improve the aesthetics and value of your home; if not, you'll only have spent 20 minutes of your life and you'll come away with a nice design, and an idea of the cost of a future upgrade. If you're thinking about having some work done at some point, get a quote and design from us. It's just a comparison, you don't have to take it – you literally have nothing to lose.'* It was just presenting things in a different way – a more relaxed way – and I really enjoyed it.

When I look at all the different parts of my life – buying a car, selling my house, eating out, going on holiday, or my next purchase – I generally buy from people I like. If you have a passion for what you do that will come through, and people will listen and maybe respond to it.

It got to the point where after the first month, I was earning more money doing telesales two nights a week than I was working full-time with the Civil Service. *So,* I thought, *Let's do it properly.* I left the CSA and went full-time in telesales.

I lasted for six months – it quickly got to the point where it was too repetitive and it wasn't challenging enough, especially when I was doing it all day. It's pretty obvious why, looking back, but

I was only 20 at the time. I've come to realise that typically, with sales, you should only do a maximum of three to four hours of the same activity at a time, or you'll end up getting a little bit bored and despondent. I always need a lot of stimulation to keep my grey matter buzzing and keep me moving forward. It was time to take stock again.

I wanted to do something that would challenge me. I loved sales and I loved targets. There had to be other jobs out there that involved both. I looked around and that's when I came across recruitment for the first time. Like a proper recruiter, I researched it as an industry and thought, *I really like the sound of this*. I didn't know anyone who did it – most of my friends were at university at the time – but I had a gut instinct that this might be for me.

My life was about to change.

Chapter Two:
The Recruitment Industry –
A Brief Overview

'Seek out opportunity and seize it.' – Deborah Meaden

This book has been written for anyone in recruitment. Whether you've just started in your first job, or you've been working as a consultant for a few years already and want to develop your skills to fulfil your potential, I can guarantee this book will help you.

My aim has been to produce the book that I wish I'd been handed when I began my recruitment career. It draws on everything I've learned in 20 years as a top recruiter – a Limitless Recruiter – and now as a Managing Director and leader in the industry I love. Used correctly, this book will save you a lot of time and headaches. It will get you from A to B quicker, and with more success (it might make you a lot of money, too). It will show you that there are no limits to what you can achieve in recruitment if you have the right mindset and adopt the right practices and techniques. All I ask of you is that you read it carefully and with an open mind, and practice the techniques I explain to you. If you do, you will reap the rewards, I promise.

Let's begin with an overview of the industry.

THE RECRUITMENT INDUSTRY
The recruitment industry as we know it today originated during the

Second World War, believe it or not! Men and women joining the war effort left gaps in the workplace and staffing agencies were set up to fill them. After the war, professional job 'recruiters' turned their efforts to finding positions for returning soldiers, tracking new vacancies from newspaper ads. Over the next decade, the curriculum vitae (that's a CV to you and me) emerged as a smart and efficient way of showcasing an individual's talents to prospective employers.

Recruitment could be slow and drawn-out until the arrival of computers, and the Internet speeded everything up enormously and turned it into the business we know and love. Despite the challenges posed by the global recession, pandemic and changes in technology, the recruitment industry continues to grow at an incredible pace. The industry is in good health. Just look at these UK figures.

THE UK RECRUITMENT INDUSTRY
– SOME FACTS AND FIGURES

- In 2019, there were over 30,000 recruitment agencies in the UK and the industry as a whole was worth over £42 billion to the UK economy
- In terms of GVA (Gross Value Added), the staffing industry was worth more to the economy than many other sectors, including the entire arts, entertainment and recreation sector (£30.7 billion) and the motor vehicle and other transport equipment manufacturing industry (£27.9 billion)
- The recruitment industry employed nearly 120,000 people
- Temporary and contract business achieved 89 per cent of the market share, or £37.8 billion

- Permanent placements accounted for £4.5 billion (11 per cent) of the market share
- On any given day in 2019, there were over 985,000 temporary and contract workers on assignment.

(All facts and figures taken from the Recruitment and Employment Confederation (REC) UK recruitment industry status report, 2019–2020).

So, what is recruitment? Broadly and simply, it's the process of *finding a suitable candidate for a job vacancy*. Why would a company use a recruitment agency to fill its vacancies? Because it can save them time, money and a lot of hassle – when it's done properly. The expertise that a good recruitment agency will provide in finding and presenting the right candidates for interview is a valuable resource. I'm the Managing Director of a recruitment agency and even I use a specialist agency to recruit staff for me.

TYPES OF RECRUITMENT

There are many different types of recruitment. The most commonplace are briefly defined below. I'm assuming that if you're interested or involved in recruitment, you'll have some familiarity with these terms. We'll be examining each in more depth later.

Permanent Recruitment – can be broadly split into three categories:

1. *Contingency Recruitment* – Contingency, or contingent,

recruitment is so called because whether a recruitment agency is paid a fee by a client is *contingent* on them filling the client's vacancy. If successful, the agency will usually be paid a percentage of the candidate's starting salary. In contingency recruitment, a recruitment agency will also often find themselves in competition with other agencies and the client's HR department.

2. *Retained Recruitment* – the recruiter will charge an upfront fee (often higher than in contingency recruitment) to the client to conduct a search, usually on an exclusive basis. Once the recruiter has head-hunted suitable candidates, the client will be invoiced at the shortlist stage and then charged once more – either when an offer has been made or on the start date of the successful candidate. Executive Search is an example of this kind of recruitment.

3. *In-House Recruitment* – also called *Internal Recruitment* – is where the recruitment function is carried out by internal recruiters, usually a division working with or from within the HR department.

Temporary Recruitment – includes all forms of non-permanent recruitment, including fixed-term assignments, contracts and project work, and ongoing temporary employment to cover such situations as maternity leave, sickness and increased workloads.

Recruitment Process Outsourcing (RPO) – this is when a company transfers all or part of its recruitment activity to an external provider. The external provider may work on site, alongside the company's HR department, for instance.

JAMES KINGSTON

RECRUITMENT – SECTORS AND ROLES

Sectors

There are recruitment agencies for pretty much every sector of industry and for every kind of job going, nowadays – from acting through to zoology. Some sectors attract more recruitment agencies than others. These include Information Technology (IT), Teaching, Energy (Renewables, Oil and Gas), Accountancy and Finance, Construction, Engineering, Manufacturing, Driving, Industrial and Healthcare, to name just a few. Then there is the massive High Street or Commercial sector, which recruits for vacancies in the above categories and any other positions a business may have, including reception, admin, sales, marketing and office support.

The High Street sector is the most visible part of the industry, with city-centre branches encouraging walk-in candidates and nationwide companies utilising large marketing budgets to raise brand awareness. Their approach is completely different to the more specialist agencies. High street agencies need more of a local and regional presence. They need to be able to respond quickly. If you're catering for the kind of role where a lot of the candidates might actually be working on or around the High Street, or the skill set isn't quite as specialised, then you need to be more visible – you need to be *on* the street. Like an estate agency, they thrive on walk-in traffic and regional brand awareness. If this sounds as though I regard the High Street agencies as second-rate, that's certainly not the case. Mrs. K. has been a director of a commercial agency for many years, and an extremely accomplished and successful one at that!

THE ART OF RECRUITMENT

Anyone can go into any recruitment sector without prior experience if they've got the right motivation. It's just a matter of understanding the idiosyncrasies of that sector, learning the processes common to all forms of recruitment and gaining experience. When I started out, most consultants were expected to come in as a 360-degree recruiter and were thrown in at the deep end – dealing with clients, candidates, vacancies and business development from the get-go. I had no real knowledge of the industry I was recruiting for, and looking back, it was a mad way to enter the business. Luckily, at that time, there were loads of vacancies to be filled (similar to the market we're in now, actually) and not a huge amount of competition, so clients gave more time and leeway, and probably tolerated rookie errors in a way they simply wouldn't today. Plus, I swam pretty good and I would never stop until I got what I wanted.

Recruitment Roles – Starting Out

Today, if you are just beginning your recruitment career, then no matter who you're working for, you'll probably start out by sourcing candidates. Resourcing is a great first step into recruitment. You begin by learning about the candidates and what they do. You'll identify and source suitable candidates for potential positions, prepare CVs, interview candidates with a range of experience and take references for them. You'll identify skills and match them with vacancies, network and advertise to attract new candidates, and generally offer a supportive admin role to more senior consultants. All the time you should be watching, listening and learning. You'll notice that some people prefer temporary contract work for the variety it can bring and the lifestyle it offers, whereas others prefer the security of a permanent job – they may have more ambition to climb the career ladder. You also learn to distinguish good candidates from bad ones.

From studying the candidates, you'll learn about the different types of employer and where they sit in an organisation. The training is, or should be, geared to make sure that when you're finally entrusted with contacting a valued client, you'll be doing so with the confidence that comes from knowing their business and what types of people would add value to it. This not only puts you in a position of strength but makes your life, as well as the client's, so much easier. It also gives you a greater chance of success.

If you're entering Executive Search then you'll probably start off as a researcher, which is similar to a resourcer, but at a more senior level. Because Executive Search is broadly concerned with recruiting for high-level, often commercially sensitive positions, there is an attention to detail in which most High Street, high-volume agencies simply cannot afford to indulge.

An Executive Search researcher will produce everything the consultants for whom they are working need to know to do their jobs effectively. Inch-thick reports of market analysis, competitor company information and detailed candidate profiles. It's a slower, more methodical way of working than that required in a High Street agency. But then, as a rule of thumb, the higher the salary, the fewer people there will be available to fill it and so it should be expected that the process may be harder and take longer.

From working as a researcher or a resourcer, you'll probably progress to becoming a consultant, then work your way up to senior consultant – managing key accounts and responsible for consistently delivering the month in, month out fees required at this level. From there the roles will vary, depending on the type and size of agency you are working for and your levels of success.

RECRUITMENT TRENDS

Technology

Recruitment is not a static industry. Like every other aspect of life, changes in technology impact on it massively. When I joined my first agency in 2002, recruitment was a very different beast. Emails and the Internet were both in their infancy and it was still commonplace for agencies to present candidates to clients by faxing their CVs or describing them over the phone. Back then, there was no LinkedIn or Google, so finding out who worked at a company was a matter of either picking up the phone and asking or walking into reception and finding out on the ground.

More recently, recruiters thought that social media was going to have a terrible effect on the recruitment industry. In fact, it has made a lot of useful tools available to savvy recruiters, who can use them to identify, connect and reach many more people, more quickly. It's so much easier now to network and find out who works where in a particular company. Some companies even post an organisational chart, or organigram, on their website, detailing who works where for them, with contact information. Any good resourcer or researcher can produce the entire structure of a company within an hour or so, thanks to the Internet and its search functions.

Back in the old days, this might have taken weeks. I had to pick up the phone and ask the receptionist, *'Who does this or that job?'* Incidentally, I still encourage my staff to do this, because it's often the quickest and most efficient way to find a specific person (not all website and online networking platforms are accurate) and you want to build up relationships with the company gatekeepers, too, which we'll cover later on.

There's no doubt that technology has simplified many aspects of recruitment. When texting and email became available, I could instantly contact a hundred candidates with the details of a vacancy, rather than having to phone them one by one and leave messages.

So, the recruitment process has speeded up – massively. The downside is that it's made it easier for all your potential competitors, too, and it has also made it easier for companies to recruit for themselves. Many organisations use social media very effectively – to develop their branding, raise their profile and encourage candidates to approach them directly through services like LinkedIn and job boards.

High-ranking job boards like Indeed and Jobsite are often the first point of call for candidates actively looking for a new position, whereas pre-Internet, they might simply have dropped into their nearest recruitment agency or turned to the jobs section of their local newspaper. More often than not, the best candidates aren't actively looking for a job – so being able to implement a passive candidate strategy is something every Limitless Recruiter should always be doing. An upside of this is that you won't be fighting over their details with another group of recruiters.

Cycles

Recruitment tends to be a cyclical process. There's usually a shortage of candidates or jobs, depending on the state of the economy. In the early 2000s, it was easy to get jobs – the economy was buoyant, and everyone was looking for staff. All I had to do was pick up the phone to a client and say,

'I recruit' and they'd reply,

'Great, I need a manager tomorrow – please get me one.' I exaggerate, but you get the idea. The difficulty then was finding candidates. They were the most valuable commodity in the industry, not jobs or clients. So 'success' became a question of how well you could locate and persuade a good candidate to consider taking a job with your client. Clients were a lot more flexible about the kind of people they would employ. You'd rarely have to negotiate hard over terms and conditions, rates or hourly mark-ups. It was a licence to print money, my old boss would say. Competition was fierce but only from a handful of agencies.

Then the market became completely saturated. Everyone has a lot of competitors in their sector – ranging from great to incompetent. The 2007–08 recession made a lot of industries re-evaluate how much they were spending on recruitment and how they did it. As a result of mass redundancies and halted projects, there was suddenly an influx of active candidates. Companies stopped investing in growth and started playing a waiting game, which meant that fewer permanent staff were getting hired. Every company became leaner. We saw more Preferred Supplier Lists (PSLs) and internal recruitment. Clients were squeezing and squeezing their recruitment budgets. Fees were negotiated a lot harder. The barometer swung the other way. A few years on, the pandemic struck and the impact on recruitment has never been so extreme in such a short space of time. Recruitment is cyclical, but there will always be opportunities if you're smart enough to spot them.

Preferred Supplier List (PSL) – *as the name suggests, a list agreed by senior management of the recruitment agencies that the company will use to find staff. It is also used to deter unwanted advances from agencies not on the list. Important to note the 'P' stands for 'Preferred'… it's not always a closed door.*

Demographics

The other big change I've noticed since entering recruitment is in demographics. Practically everyone who applies to join my company is a graduate these days – that was rare 20 years ago, and almost unheard of 40 years ago. And when I first started visiting construction companies, the only place you'd see a woman was at the front desk. Now many firms are targeting to get to 50 per cent female employment in the future. Diversity is an important issue for most employers to consider, and rightly so.

Companies are also more conscious of the need to attract the best employees than perhaps they used to be and so they go out of their way to make the workplace an appealing environment: the fact that in 2021, 'work-life balance' is currently top of the list for talent seeking a new role just highlights how much the world has changed in recruitment.

Of course, you have to use all these changes to your advantage, or you'll lag behind. It's all very well having access to every book in the library, but you need to make time to read them. It's easier to analyse useful data quickly now. We can routinely check where our candidate flow is coming from – geographically, by sector, by position – and also where our CVs originate from. This helps us to target our advertising spend. We produce a salary survey every year, which is helpful to candidates and companies – to make sure they're not falling behind and they know where to pitch jobs or salary demands. The good recruiter's USP isn't databases anymore – it's knowledge. And as my first mentor always said, '*In recruitment, knowledge is power.*'

THE LIMITLESS RECRUITER KNOWS THAT…

- **In 2019, there were over 30,000 recruitment agencies in the UK**
- **The UK sector is worth nearly £42 billion and is more valuable to the economy than many other sectors, including the arts, entertainment and recreation sector, and the motor vehicle and other transport equipment manufacturing industry**
- **The UK recruitment industry employs over 119,000 people**
- **Recruitment tends to be a cyclical process**
- **Legislation is constantly changing the way agencies and clients work.**

Chapter Three:
Know Your Industry

'Stay calm, stay focused, work with the people around you, share the strain, find the solution. Give yourself a chance, not a coronary.'
– James Caan, entrepreneur and 'Dragon's Den' celebrity.

Whether you're moving into recruitment or you feel that it's time for a change of sector, you need to do your research. Recruitment is all about the knowledge. You really need to have a reason to want to work in a particular sector, but you should also learn to think more widely about different markets – to develop an industry overview. So, look at where money is being invested in the wider economy. Next, what percentage is the GDP of that sector in the economy? Think about how things like Brexit, or the pandemic, might potentially affect different parts of the industry. What are the biggest challenges facing your chosen sector? Is labour an issue? How many companies are in that sector, delivering the same thing? What's the scope for growth and opportunity? Do your research.

THE BEST BIT OF ADVICE BEFORE STARTING A CAREER IN RECRUITMENT
While there's no golden rule that decides whether someone is going to be a good recruiter in a certain sector or not, there is an early warning for someone with a little self-knowledge: if you're

thin-skinned and not goal-orientated, then recruitment might not be the best industry for you. This is why, when we're interviewing fresh-faced young graduates who might never have had a job, we know it's a gamble.

Recruitment is Marmite – you'll probably either love it or hate it. In my experience, after two years of working in the industry someone will either be in it for life or looking for a path out. Recruitment is hard. It's different and it's very challenging, but it's also one of the most rewarding industries in every way. The industry average used to be that one out of four trainee recruiters left within two years because they just couldn't deal with the targets, environment, frustrations and repeated rejection. It all comes down to mindset. The best consultants, the Limitless Recruiters, aren't always the ones who can consistently deliver – that's just a utopia – they're the ones who recognise that a bad day is just part of the process, put it behind them and quickly move on to the next challenge.

The Limitless Recruiter recognises that a bad day in recruitment is just part of the process, not the end of the world.' – James Kingston

---

CHOOSE THE RIGHT SECTOR FOR YOU

To work out which sector of recruitment you should work in, consider the kind of person you are. This isn't as obvious as it may seem. For instance, privately-educated, well-spoken technical applicants often end up working in our consultancy division, where they're interacting with people from the same background. Birds of a feather flock together. On the other hand, another key to success is being memorable. Someone with the right skill set and mindset, but not from the same background as their clients and candidates, can really stand out and make an impression.

Starting out, ask yourself: what kind of people do you get on with? What kind of people do you relate to? As a chatterbox and an extrovert, I feel equally comfortable talking with directors, consultants and the person who's on the front desk or sweeping up. And it's no doubt true that a really good recruiter is also a bit of a chameleon, someone who can adapt to their environment.

Ideally, you'll have a bit of a passion for a sector to succeed in it. When I decided I wanted to try recruitment, I looked around and narrowed my choices down to three sectors – Information Technology (IT), Finance and Construction.

Finance wasn't a sector I knew much about and the job specifications didn't thrill me. What I learned about IT was that I probably wouldn't feel much empathy with the candidates. I had nothing against them at all, but I just wasn't like them. It's important to be able to identify and relate with the people you'll be spending a lot of time with and looking to help through their careers.

By contrast, I was fascinated by what I learned about the construction sector and the people in it. Construction had gone through a recession in the 1990s, and it was coming out of that and actually quite buoyant by the early 2000s. There was a Labour government, which wanted to build lots of schools and hospitals.

THE ART OF RECRUITMENT

There was such a vast range of roles in construction – from people labouring on sites, to architects who designed the buildings, to the directors of FTSE 100 major construction companies who were making massive investment decisions and helping to shape the landscape we see around us today. The variety of the sector made it a challenge and compelling to me. Other people hate having that variety of personality types to deal with – they prefer more consistency and predictability, and there's nothing wrong with that. Recruiting for the same few positions day in, day out wouldn't suit me – but it might suit you. There is no right and wrong with this. It's about knowing the type of person you are. Ask yourself, why are you doing the job? What gets you out of bed? Identify your motivation and then marry it to the right sector to recruit in.

If you're coming into recruitment from a particular sector – if you've worked in construction, the oil industry or accountancy, and know it well – then that might be the place to start. Your sector needs to be a mirror of you. If you have an interest or passion in it then people will see that. Success come from passion and a belief in your product, and your product is people.

Different sectors have different cycles – different peaks and troughs. When I joined Hill McGlynn (now Randstad) as a construction consultant, they asked me,

'Do you like summer holidays?' I said.

'Yeah.' They said.

'Well, you won't anymore.'

Summers are absolutely flat out in construction recruitment, certainly for freelance consultants, and you don't want to miss out on any opportunity. In fact, freelance recruitment is very fast-paced in general. If you don't know your market – keep tabs on every job, every project, every client, every candidate – you'll lose control of it. On the other hand, if you like Christmas then construction is a great sector to work in. Nothing happens. But then Christmas is hell-for-leather in catering and High Street recruitment, because that's when people are off doing their shopping and celebrating, so seasonal staff are in great demand.

Starting out with a big, well-known agency has advantages and disadvantages. It can be easier to make placements because of access to candidates, the spend on advertising and the company profile. You might also find it constricting, because the company will have more branches, each covering a smaller patch. I remember feeling frustrated at my first agency when a client I had a close relationship with asked me to recruit for a position based in another county. Because of the agency rules, I had to hand it over to another branch, who then reaped the benefits.

Bigger doesn't necessarily mean better if you're ambitious, but it's a good place to learn. A company with a high profile, more marketing spend and good training might seem an easier place to start. But a smaller agency could be more exciting and offer greater opportunities for quick progression and learning directly from the most senior people in the business. I have a recruiter working for me who could have gone to any major agency, but chose to come here and set up a new division from scratch – a whole new market. He's now a director and shareholder in the business, manages a team and is reaping the benefits. But he's also quickly become a key person in our business – a big cog in a smaller wheel.

So, a big agency can be a good place to begin your career. On the other hand, if you can get in with a good, small agency where you'll get direct training from someone like me, then frankly that's going to be a hundred times better – if you have the ambition.

The same goes for the type of recruitment you should be doing. If you're a bit of a chess player by nature, a bit slower and more methodical, and pay attention to every detail, then permanent recruitment might best suit your temperament. If you're able to plug gaps, love juggling a lot of balls in the air, like quick wins and respond immediately to a crisis, then you may have the skillset for temporary or freelance recruitment. The chances are that if you spend a number of years developing your career you'll end up doing both, but try and go for the type of recruitment that suits your personality better as a starting-point.

Some people find they are happier as a resourcer or researcher than as a consultant or business developer, because they don't like cold-calling clients. They might go into internal recruitment for a company where they'll be in a less sales-driven environment. Their earning potential may decrease as a result, but if they are happier in the work they do then they've made the right decision. Different environments and challenges suit different personalities.

DO YOUR RESEARCH

I had a mentor at my first agency. He was an ex-construction manager and hard as nails, but he was also very wise. He told me that the key to having a good recruitment career is to treat it like a building project. If you do the right things at the start – learn your sector and market, and don't cut corners – you'll build a strong foundation that will offer you security and strength. Put all the blocks in place first and then you can keep building your career. Meet as many candidates as possible, get to know their jobs inside out and what makes them tick. Take thorough references. If you don't know your market, if you don't know the industry and you place bad people – the equivalent of using cheap and shoddy materials – then your career will come crashing down around you.

And this is the biggest problem for a lot of recruiters – they're so financially driven that they don't care about how they make the money – they just care about making placements. They don't care about vetting candidates, or whether someone is really suitable or not. For me that's not what recruitment is all about. That way, you quickly lose candidate and client trust. Those who come into recruitment just looking for the money, who are willing to take short cuts for short-term gains, tend to be short-lived and often get despondent. Very quickly.

Knowledge is everything. Detail is everything. For instance, you might speak to two people in different companies with the same job title, but doing completely different roles. One project manager's responsibilities may be completely unlike another's. This is where a lot of consultants fall down – their inability to grasp what their clients do, and therefore be able to give them what they need. The Limitless Recruiter will always have a handle on this.

Knowing and understanding what each role means and what will make someone a good or a bad fit at a particular company, or for a particular client, and being able to find that person – that is what makes the difference.

When anyone wants to join my company, they have to give me a presentation about the sector they will be working in. Whether they've worked in recruitment before or not, we get them to go away and research the sector, all the different roles in the sector, what each person does, what their career path is, how much they earn and therefore potential fees, how many companies employ these different roles and how many of each they have. This knowledge is crucial to their own development as a recruitment consultant. It's not enough to know just what someone does, but also how they do it – how they make their money and how you can add value to that. Once you know this you can really *consult* with them. I'll go and see a client now and say, *'We can create roles for you to help you win business, or improve health and safety, or operational delivery, based on my experience across the industry over 20 years'.* I know not only what they do and how they do it, but their place in the market and how their competitors operate. That knowledge is priceless to a client.

NEW SECTORS

Whenever we go into a new sector that I don't know anything about, the first question I ask is, *'How big is the canvas for this sector, before we start trying to paint on it?'* There's nothing to stop a consultant recruiting for a sector UK-wide, or even internationally, but we always say, *'Go where you can see people'.* The key to good recruitment is building relationships and that means going to see people face-to-face.

With that in mind, let's say we're considering whether it's worth recruiting for the Space Engineering sector in the South West region. I need to find out how many potential clients there are in the area and then how many people each of those potential clients employs – that gives you an immediate idea of the value and viability of the sector. If there are a thousand companies in Space Engineering and its supply chain, that tells you there's a lot of potential. If there are only five or ten in the whole region, where are the candidates going to come from? Is there enough potential in the market to make lots of placements, and grow and develop?

So whenever I look at a market, that's the first thing I consider – how big is the opportunity? If it's there, then we start to paint and fill in the canvas. In order to paint, you need to do your research – who's growing, who's shrinking, who's plateauing in that sector.

If you're thinking of joining a new recruitment agency or sector, you need to consider these things and then you need to find out how many other agencies and consultants are already recruiting for the sector you are interested in. If there are a lot, is that off-putting? Possibly, but it also might mean there's a lot of potential for a really good recruiter. If a bigger agency is setting up a division in a new sector, it's a sign that they've seen something developing in the market. Never stop learning about the sector, never stop researching.

THE RIGHT AGENCY FOR YOU

Okay, so you've decided which sector you want to work in or move to. Now you need to select agencies to apply to. You may have been impressed by one already, if you work in the same sector, but if not, there are some shortcuts you can take in compiling a shortlist. Treat it like a police investigation, with you as the lead detective.

First, take **a five-minute tour of the agency's website** – they have a website, right? Look for accreditations and membership of industry bodies. They should be a member of a recruitment body working to the highest standards in British recruitment. If the website was last updated sometime last year, that's a sure sign they're not very busy (unless it's the first week of January). You should see new vacancies from the past seven days, and preferably a recent blog about the company itself or the wider industry. Look through their **online vacancies** to make sure the roles they recruit for broadly match your ambitions.

If you're keen to work for a specialist recruiter, rather than a High Street agency, **read through blogs, articles and their team profiles** – assuming they have them. Look for their insights about their sector and recruitment in general. Start making judgements. Client testimonials are not only a clear indication of the recruiter's contacts, but also show that employers value the agency's work enough to say so to the world.

Next, **search social media** to see if the agency's profiles are up to date or neglected. Any business with something worth shouting about will shout about it. Google them, looking for links from employers, positive user reviews and industry awards. See how they are ranked and rated on company comparison sites like Glassdoor.

Take notes while you're doing this – especially if you are compiling a shortlist with a few agencies on it. It may otherwise be difficult to remember which agency did what later on.

When you're ready to make contact, be aware of every aspect of the agency's response. If you're applying to an online vacancy, do they acknowledge your application in a timely and courteous manner? If you're phoning them speculatively to see if they have any recruiter vacancies, how does the receptionist answer your call? Are you connected to the right person efficiently? If they promise a reply by email, does it come when they promised? How is it formatted? Overall, how does the company come across – professional or sloppy? Chances are, whatever impression they give you, that's how clients and candidates feel about them, too; and you'll be seen in the same light if you start working for them.

First Impressions

So, you have been invited for an interview. Congratulations! Keep your wits about you when you attend. Rather than focusing on your nerves – and you should have some – concentrate on your first impressions as you walk in the door. What's the office like? Is it smart or are there stains on the wall? Is the receptionist professional and welcoming, or does he or she ignore you? Is there a buzz in the office? Can you hear lots of happy voices on the phone, or is it like a morgue at midnight? Again, remember that this is what candidates, and possibly clients, will see when they come in to meet you, if you are offered a job and decide to accept.

THE ART OF RECRUITMENT

Ten Questions to Ask at an Interview

When you're asked at the end of the interview whether you have any questions, *please make sure you have some ready to ask*. Not only is it in your interest to find out as much as you can about the place you're potentially going to be spending a lot of your waking hours in, but it shows the interviewer that you're taking the interview seriously. Also, having an enquiring and probing mind are essential prerequisites for any successful recruiter. People who don't ask questions when they come to us for an interview don't get asked back. Here are some questions you might want to ask, but please do the research and think of your own:

1. What career progression do you offer? *Are you there to make up the numbers – cannon fodder – or are you there to make a difference?*
2. What's the training structure like? *How much time and effort do they invest in their staff – remember, that could include you.*
3. What's your USP in the market? *If they don't know, politely curtail the interview – they're wasting your time.*
4. What's your average margin (on freelance and temporary contracts) and what's the average permanent placement fee? *Are they over- or under-charging? Are they at market average? The answer will tell you a lot about how they're performing.*
5. What are your biggest challenges at the moment – candidate generation, or finding vacancies? *This should tell you how honest they are. If they say, 'Neither', don't believe them.*
6. What does your number one consultant earn, and what does your average biller make? *Well, you want to know, don't you?*

7. What is the average length of employment with you for a consultant? *Do they stick around, or head for the door as soon as they understand what's going on?*

8. What's your five-year plan? *If they don't know where they're going, how can you?*

9. What is the largest number of candidates you've placed with a particular client? *Ongoing client relationships are key to business success.*

10. What's your policy on sharing candidates? *There's nothing worse than competing against people on your own team.*

If you came for an interview with me and asked those questions, I'd be impressed. It would show that you care, that you're interested in my agency and that you are passionate about your future.

YOUR FIRST YEAR

Your first year of recruitment is always your hardest. When I started out, naturally no one had heard of me. I had no relationships with any clients. My goal was to let them know who I was, as quickly as possible. I contacted as many clients as I could. I built up relationships by talking to them, going to see them – whether onsite for a coffee or out for a beer. My goal was simply to build up my name. I looked at it as a numbers game again, just as I had in telesales. The more people you call, the more people you speak to, meet and hopefully impress, the more likely it is you'll get a vacancy to fill.

In my first week there was so much to learn. I felt overloaded with information. I'd worked in sales, so had no fear of cold-calling people, but I'd never worked in an environment like this. The systems were different, everyone was out to get one over on everyone else. There was not a lot of teamwork. As I remember it, someone told me,

'There's a phone, there's your client list, get on with it.'

To be fair, the agency had great introductory training, but they ran it every three months and I'd missed it by days. So there I was, the naïve trainee, sat between two experienced consultants who were fighting over candidates. Neither of them wanted to give me any time because they were too busy competing for commission. The consultant to my left was one of the best I've ever heard on the phone, but he didn't have a driving licence and so he never went out on company visits. The one on my right wasn't the best at building relationships on the phone, but great at developing client relationships face-to-face. So I thought, *I'll take the best of both of these*, and that's how I became James Kingston the Limitless Recruiter. I was learning from two very good consultants who had different strengths. I listened, I learned, took what they did that worked and tried to improve on things that didn't.

The beauty of recruitment is that it's process-led, once you know what you're doing. It's a numbers' game. As long as you're doing enough of these tasks, and you get better every time you do them, then you will do really, really well. So, if you have a bad day, it will even up and always get better. That's the highs and lows of recruitment – tears one day, champagne the next!

THE LIMITLESS RECRUITER WILL...
- Work out which sector of recruitment they should be working in by considering the kind of person they are
- Know that knowledge is everything, detail is everything
- Never stop researching and learning about their chosen sector
- Realise that recruitment is a process – you need to learn it to succeed
- Understand that success comes from passion and a belief in your product, and your product is people.

PART TWO: MASTERING THE RECRUITMENT PROCESS

Step by step and the thing is done.' – Charles Atlas

Recruitment is, above all else, a process. It doesn't matter which sector you're working in – IT, Finance, High Street, Construction – there are certain steps you have to follow to succeed. Once you understand this, and master all the activities, you'll be well on your way to becoming a Limitless Recruiter.

The next three chapters will dissect the whole process stage-by-stage (listed below) and show you how to excel in every area. Whether you are a new or experienced consultant, this section will get you looking at recruitment in ways you probably haven't before and take your abilities to the next level.

Chapter Four:
The Candidate

'When dealing with people, remember you are not dealing with creatures of logic, but creatures of emotion.' – Dale Carnegie

"In the world of recruitment, your most valuable asset is your candidate." – James Kingston

- Candidate Generation
- Writing and Designing Job Adverts
- Candidate Registration
- Taking References
- CV Writing and Candidate Profiling

Candidates, it should hardly need saying, are just as important as clients. After all, without them you'll have nothing to trade or talk to your clients about. And as with clients, building good relationships with candidates is vital. If you're working in temporary and freelance recruitment, your candidates will (hopefully) fill more than one assignment for you. You'll need to get to know their likes and dislikes, their attributes and flaws, so that you can represent them in the best light to clients, but also keep them happy and working – for you.

Equally, candidates you place in permanent vacancies have a value that lasts well beyond the recruitment fee. They indirectly represent you and your agency. This starts with the impression they make at interview stage, but continues after their successful placement. They will talk about you and your agency to colleagues – either recommending you or being uncomplimentary about you, depending on the service they've received. Some of them will rise through the ranks and become clients, so you want them to remember you for all the right reasons. A candidate with a positive experience of your services is a hundred times more effective than any business development you can do.

CANDIDATE GENERATION

To have a database of candidates, you need to attract them to your agency. There are two types of candidate generation – active and passive.

Active Candidate Generation

These are candidates who are already on the market, actively seeking new employment. They're contacting agencies or applying directly to companies through job boards or company websites. You have to work fast with these candidates. If they're not satisfied by your approach, it won't be long before they look elsewhere. I have consultants who only really put themselves out for this – the vacancy-led candidate. This is understandable, but it's a mistake. You will never become a Limitless Recruiter by restricting your options in this way.

Passive Candidate Generation

These candidates are in roles already and are not actively seeking something new. Such people are often the best candidates. You need to get yourself in front of them. Why? Think about it this way. Imagine if you spent a little time identifying the best candidates in your region for a particular role in your sector. Then you kept in touch with them on a regular basis. Who do you think they'll get in touch with when they *are* looking for a new position?

There are pros and cons to passive candidate generation. On the plus side, because they're not on the market they are exclusively yours, as far as their interest extends. On the negative side, this means they potentially come with a lot of baggage – they may not be so committed and ready to jump when a great opportunity arises. It's passive candidates who tend to attract the highest number of counter-offers from their current employers and they have the largest drop-out rate, too.

Candidate Strategy
Every consultant needs a really strong candidate strategy – a mix of active and passive generation. I can't emphasise enough that a whole-of-the-market approach is vital if you want to be a Limitless Recruiter. It means you have a constant flow of fresh candidates available, which allows you to cover every angle of recruitment – from vacancy-led to the speculative marketing of candidates, or 'speccing out'.

Many recruiters won't bother looking beyond their own databases or a job board for candidates. This means they're missing out on over half the candidates in the market. At the moment, we're in a market where people are struggling to find candidates. Unemployment is at a 44-year low, with a record number of people being employed in the UK, so you have to think of innovative ways to attract candidates to your agency.

The point is that the best people often aren't looking for a job at the time when you're looking to fill it. This especially applies to more senior positions – the roles for which you might head-hunt, for instance. Roles where there is a lack of really good candidates, because of the specialist knowledge or experience required. These placements often pay very well, so it's worth making the effort. Your job is to find that needle in the haystack.

"The best recruiters always have a proactive candidate strategy."
– James Kingston

Candidate Sourcing

There are many ways to source candidates. I often ask my consultants, *'Where are your future candidates now? Where would they go to find a job? How did they find the job they're in?'* Think like they do. If you're an office manager, what media will you browse to see what opportunities are out there? Might you ask a colleague? If you're a nurse, how will you find your next promotion? If you're working in IT, do you look in different places to someone who works in retail? Of course you do. So as a consultant, you need to put yourself in your candidates' shoes. We analyse on a regular basis where our candidates are coming from, so that we can maximise our advertising effectiveness. I've listed some sources below:

THE ART OF RECRUITMENT

- Referrals
- Direct applications (e.g. through a website)
- Direct sourcing/head-hunting
- Job boards (CV databases and applications)
- Existing database
- Professional/social networking platforms – LinkedIn, Facebook
- Mailshots
- Media advertising, including regional/ national newspapers
- Networking – open evenings and corporate events
- Out-sourcing
- Job centres
- Client visits
- References
- Awards/accreditation websites.

Again, the Limitless Recruiter will be constantly thinking outside the box. Whenever you talk to a client about a vacancy, ask them where they found their last candidate – it might give you a clue as to where to look this time.

At least 25 per cent of the candidates we fill vacancies with come from referrals by other candidates or clients who have happily worked with us in the past. Whether you are looking to attract fresh-faced university graduates with the right qualifications, or a managing director for an aerospace engineering company with 20 years' relevant experience, the point is that you need to target your advertising to attract them. Through networking platforms, by direct approach, a mailshot: whatever works best from past attempts. Or try something completely new. Different vacancies have different candidate generation parameters, but the key takeaway is that the best recruiters always have a proactive candidate strategy.

There are two or three disciplines for which we recruit regularly. It's the same for any agency, regardless of sector. I've always got adverts out for these positions and my consultants identify and keep in touch with the best candidates we're aware of in each discipline, regardless of whether they are looking for a job at the moment.

Recruiting in construction, for instance, we've got lists of project managers and quantity surveyors – those who are currently employed; those who have longevity with their employer; the ones who are the best in their field. These people are at the top of their game: they win awards and are always the names recommended by others. They are the best in the market and we're talking to them on a bi-monthly basis. We want them to come to us straightaway when they're looking for a new challenge. We know we'll be able to get each of them three to five interviews when they do, and that our clients will be keen to see and hear about them.

Passive candidate head-hunting works: *'I appreciate you may not be actively looking for a new role at present, but your details have been provided to me as someone who we may, in the future, be able to help find the next step in your career. Are you happy in your current job? What would you change about your current job if you could? What type of role, if it came on the market, would you want to hear about?'* This gets them to start thinking about their situation and what it lacks. It's a different approach to active candidates where you might head-hunt them by saying, *'I've*

seen your CV online and I want to talk about a specific vacancy.'
Often, with passive candidates, we'll arrange to meet them for a coffee so they can tell us about their dream job. If we approach 16 such candidates, one in four are usually interested in meeting. Of those, one in four will agree to their CV being sent to a client for consideration. Generally, one out of 16 head-hunting calls will change a passive candidate into an active candidate. For senior positions, this method can really pay dividends.

So, candidate generation is not just about candidates responding to your website or advertisements – although these sources are obviously very important. You need to be constantly thinking, *Where are my future candidates coming from?* Not just the ones already on the market, because then you're just competing in reactive, rat-race recruitment. And how do you ensure you are the first person they call when they do start looking actively? Your information needs to be in front of them, regularly.

Recruitment is like a jigsaw puzzle. You will not succeed by being good at filling in only one part of it. You need to be looking at all parts of the picture at the same time – working on all parts of the process simultaneously – to achieve the maximum success. Some consultants will have a great quarter and then fall off a cliff. You need activity at every level all the time. You must be talking to candidates who are actively looking for a new job, but also those who are not. This is the way to become a Limitless Recruiter.

Candidate Strategy – Tips and Tricks
• If you're an experienced consultant, *have an aftercare strategy*

for previously-placed candidates. Get in touch with them. When was the last time you spoke to the first candidate you placed? How do you know they're not looking for a new position now, or hiring people themselves? Or they might know someone in their company who is on the lookout?

• *Go through previously-sent CVs for similar vacancies.* Even if you didn't place the candidates in their current job, you have a shared history and know something about them. Contact them to see if they might be interested in a new opportunity, or know someone they can recommend.

• Ask good candidates, including ones you've already placed, to *refer a friend* they know who works in a similar position, or ask them who in their company is the best in a different role. For example, if they are in the commercial department ask them who is the best person in operations? Your agency may even be prepared to offer a small financial incentive if you place someone as a result. We have a 'refer a friend' scheme that pays up to £1,000 for every successfully-placed new candidate we were not previously aware of – win, win.

WRITING AND DESIGNING JOB ADVERTS

You have all the information about a vacancy from a client and now you want to advertise it. How you write and design the job advertisement will determine whether you attract suitable candidates. These days, you usually have a limited time-frame to attract the reader's attention before they most likely scroll down to the next job, so you have to make an immediate impact. Because of the prominence of online searches, it is equally important that you write the advert from a Search Engine Optimisation (SEO) point of view. We'll now consider both of these aspects in more detail.

Writing Job Adverts

The aim of a job advert is to attract interest, communicate the essential information and provide a clear 'call to action' to the target audience. Any branding should be proportionate and not overbearing. *Always keep in mind that the job is your product and the readers of the job advert are your potential customers.* So a well-written job advert will:

- Be eye-catching
- Maintain the reader's attention by being engaging
- Have a clear call to action.

The advert must grab the reader's attention and then keep it. The reader must be able to relate instantly to what they are seeing and reading, without feeling that they're being patronised or misled by over-the-top content and claims. Then the advert must give the potential candidate a clear 'call to action' – it's got to make them want to contact you immediately after they've finished reading it.

Job Adverts – Tips and Tricks

- *Short but visually impactful adverts* attract attention straightaway, before leading on to the detail. It is important to foreground the details about the role, or the USPs. This is especially true of ads for social media outlets like Facebook or LinkedIn, where people will often only stop scrolling if something immediately catches their attention. We often create *teaser adverts*, or job alerts, specifically designed for social media platforms. These teasers catch the eye and give just enough information to encourage potential candidates to click through to a more detailed job advert (an example of which you'll find at the end of this section). Job title, location, salary and a call to action. They are the equivalent of the mailers we send to clients and they are very cost-effective.

- *Think about where the advert is going to appear and who it is meant to appeal to.* A labourer in Bristol is going to respond to a different set of stimuli – visual and textual – to a senior executive in London. This isn't a value judgement, it's just that a labourer's vacancy spec is unlikely to contain the reams of detail that a senior executive's role might require: job title, location, salary – this is all that's required. 90 per cent of all industrial roles are filled through social media, including Facebook. That's where the candidates are – that's where their attention is. Target your audience.

- *Job adverts should follow the classic **AIDA** selling format*: Attention, Interest, Desire, Action. This means that good job adverts must first attract **Attention** (from appropriate jobseekers). This is often achieved with an eye-catching banner or headline. Next, the advert must build **Interest** by establishing its relevance in the minds of ideal candidates. The ad content must create **Desire** by emphasising the appeal of the job and the rewards which await the reader. Finally, you must prompt **Action**, which may be to call a telephone number or email a CV.

THE ART OF RECRUITMENT

- Open the advertisement with *three strong, relatable questions* that will grab the reader's attention and create interest (see the Recruitment Consultant job ad below as an example).

- Alternatively, *use one simple headline*, making it relevant and clear. Using the job title is an obvious example. When doing this, bear in mind the Search Engine Optimisation (SEO), which we'll look at later on. The job title needs to be clear and eminently searchable. If you want to recruit a jockey, use the word 'jockey', not a description like 'rider of horses,' because it's unlikely that a jockey would use such a phrase when searching for vacancies! Job boards often expect this approach, followed by a couple of short lines of description. So we might bolster our *Trainee Recruitment Consultant* teaser ad on a job board with, *'Fantastic Career Opportunity in Bristol'*.

- If the job title does not implicitly describe the job functions, *use a strap line* to do so. If you find yourself writing a job advert for a truly obscure job title – which in no way conveys what the job function is – consider changing the job title to better reflect its content.

- An effective *alternative headline* – especially for strategic roles with a lot of freedom – is to describe (briefly, and in an inspirational manner) the main purpose of the role, followed by the job title as a secondary heading.

- If the organisation is well-known and *a sought-after place to work*, then be careful not to give too much information away. Agencies always check competitors' job adverts.

- *Make the advert easy to read*. Use simple language, avoid complicated words unless absolutely necessary and leave enough space around the text to attract attention to it. Less is usually more. Efficient writing enables efficient reading.

- *Mirror the kind of language that your target reader uses.* Think about who you want to attract and what they like to read.
- *Use short sentences.* More than fifteen words in a sentence tends to reduce its clarity. After drafting your advert, edit out commas and 'ands', replacing them with full stops. Also vary sentence length. This holds the attention.
- *Use bullet points and short, bite-size paragraphs.* A lot of words in one big paragraph can be very off-putting to the reader.
- *Use simple type styles*: Arial or Arial Narrow, for instance.
- *Use 12–20 point size for headings and subheadings.* Try to avoid upper case text (capitals), even in headings. Increase prominence by the use of a larger point size and emboldening, to some extent, rather than by using capitals. CAPITALS HAVE NO WORD SHAPES – SEE WHAT I MEAN?
- *Avoid italics (in job ads!), shadows, light colours reversed out of dark, weird and wonderful colours.* All of these reduce readability. Use simple black (or dark-colour) text on a white (or light-colour) background for maximum readability.
- *Involve the reader by referring to them in the second person* – as 'you'. This helps people to visualise themselves in the role.
- *Stress what is unique.* Where appropriate, emphasise what makes the job and the organisation stand out. Some people are attracted by a company's reputation or a particular kind of role. But bear in mind that
- *Job advert statements and descriptions must be credible.*

Employers or jobs which sound too good to be true usually are, and will therefore attract only the gullible and the dreamers.

TRAINEE RECRUITMENT CONSULTANT – BRISTOL – GREAT CAREER OPPORTUNITY

Are you a motivated, confident individual looking to start your career within the recruitment industry?
Are you looking to progress quickly, earn big and benefit from expert bespoke training?
Would you like to be part of a dynamic, multi-award-winning business with a great working environment?

Then get in touch!
Kingston Barnes are currently looking for new talent to join our expanding team in Bristol. Due to continued growth, we are currently looking for several trainee recruitment consultants to join the team in our prestigious Queen Square office.

The Company
Kingston Barnes is a multi-award-winning recruitment consultancy, offering a first-class service to the Construction, Engineering and Logistics industries. We are passionate about being the best to work with and the best to work for. Rewarding and celebrating top performances, supporting our employees through expert training and promoting more fun, less politics. We look for individuals who share these values and have big ambitions for the future.

JAMES KINGSTON

The Position

As a Recruitment Consultant within Kingston Barnes, you will be responsible for attracting candidates and matching them to temporary or permanent positions for our client companies. These jobs may vary from entry-level roles to senior management. You will build relationships with clients in order to gain a better understanding of their recruitment needs and requirements. You will attract candidates by producing job adverts in a wide range of media, as well as by networking, head-hunting and through referrals. You will also be required to screen candidates, interview them, conduct background checks and match candidates to clients. This is a sales role, where you will be encouraged to meet people face-to-face.

The successful trainee will be invited to join a 12-week hands-on trainee programme, where you will learn the full process of recruitment: from referencing and interviewing candidates to visiting clients and taking a detailed vacancy, shortlisting candidates and arranging interviews. During this time, you will have the support of a mentor to guide you through the process. You will also be given invaluable experience as you spend time with our clients, learning about the industry we are passionate to recruit for.

What We Offer:

On-Target Earnings (OTE) (£25–35k in the first year)

Recognition and rewards with regular incentives, including days out, dinner at Michelin star restaurants and our annual company ski trip

Bespoke first-class training and continuous personal development

Being a part of one of the fastest-growing businesses in the South West

A great working environment, culture and values.

What's Required

The ideal candidate will be ambitious and hungry for good career progression – a success-driven individual who works hard in order to achieve results. As this is a sales environment, previous experience is beneficial, though not completely necessary. As long as you are resilient and energetic, we want to hear from you.

As a 360-degree consultant you will be dealing with clients and candidates, so a confident client-facing persona is a must. Kingston Barnes prides itself on offering a far superior service to our clients than its competitors.

If you are interested in applying to become part of Kingston Barnes, please send a copy of your CV to office@kingstonbarnes.com or contact us on 0117 325 2233 to discuss further.

Job Advert 'No-No's

Here are some common mistakes made by inexperienced consultants when designing and writing job adverts. You'll come across them on job boards all the time. To become a Limitless Recruiter, follow my tips and avoid these gaffs. You will end up with strong, readable, interesting ads. Bad adverts often

• *Are difficult to read quickly*, or at all

- *Use a font (type, style) that is too small or too large*
- *Use a lot of* CAPITAL LETTERS
- *Are printed in dark colours or tints* against a coloured, patterned or picture background
- Feature *clever or obscure headlines*
- *Contain too much technical detail* about the job or the company
- *Contain too many words* – a real turn-off. Keep it simple!
- Feature *uninspiring, tedious descriptions* of roles and ideal candidates
- Place *too much emphasis on the job and not enough on the person.*

Job Adverts Checklist

Keeping in mind the writing and design tips above, here are the items to include in an effective job advert:

- Job title
- Name of the agency or consultancy
- Job location
- Brief description of business/organisation activity, their market position and aims
- Indication of where the role is in the company structure, and who the candidate will report to
- Outline of the job role and purpose
- Indication of the scale, size, responsibility, timescale and territory of the role
- Brief profile of the ideal candidate – expressed in the 'second person' (you, your, etc.)

- Indication of qualifications and experience required (which could be incorporated within the candidate profile)
- Salary (or salary guide)
- Whether the role is full-time, permanent or a short-term contract (if not explicitly clear from elsewhere in the advert)
- Other package details (pension, car, etc.)
- Response and application instructions
- Your contact details
- Job and specific advert reference (advert references help you analyse results from different adverts for the same job).

Keywords and Search Engine Optimisation (SEO) of Job Adverts

Search Engine Optimisation (SEO) – Search Engine Optimisation is the process of increasing the number of visitors to a webpage or website by obtaining a high-ranking placement in the search results of a search engine such as Google.

To ensure any kind of success with online job adverts, you have to be aware of SEO factors that will influence whether ads rise up the list of pages, to attract a lot of attention, or sink without trace in a results black hole. Books have been written on this subject alone, so there is only room for some quick tips in passing here. While it will likely be only a small part of your role as a consultant (most larger companies do not allow consultants access to SEO procedures), it's an interesting subject and one that it will pay dividends to explore, especially as your career progresses and you find yourself taking on more responsibility for areas like SEO.

Keywords

Google is by far the most used search engine on the Internet, so I'll refer to it in this section. Most of you will know that a 'keyword' is what someone will type when conducting a job search on Google. For instance, a candidate looking for a recruitment consultant job in Bristol might search for 'Recruitment Job Bristol', where all three words are keywords. In order for your job vacancy to come up in Google's search results you have to match that search, or the 'keywords', with keywords written in your job vacancy advert.

When writing a job advert, don't fall into the trap of writing all about the company first. The closer to the top of your advert your keywords are placed, the more recognition your page will receive from search engines. Many search engines expect your first few sentences to be relevant to the theme of your page. So if you start by writing more about the client than you do about the vacancy, search engines may think the page is about the company rather than a project management job.

For our consultant's role, we might start the advert with something like, 'Trainee Recruitment Consultants needed to join our expanding team,' rather than 'Kingston Barnes is Looking for Consultants'. Google Ads have a useful keyword planner that evaluates your advert and can provide information about the number of monthly searches a particular keyword receives.

Google looks specifically at the following features:
• The Domain Name
• Body Text – Keywords.

Domain Name

The name of your website (the domain name) used to be a great way to boost your ranking in search results. If you sold carpets and your website name was *sellcarpets.com*, that alone might secure you prominence. Google became aware that some companies were doing little more than buying a domain name containing a keyword in order to do this, so they have made it more difficult for this method to have an impact. As a result, the following factors are more important to consider.

Body Text

Your body text should be around 500 words and should mention the vacancy, the industry and the job location several times. The body text typically contains all the content in the page: company description, job description, qualifications required and additional information. Search engines look at the content within the body text to assign the uniqueness and relevance of that content. If the page doesn't have enough words, search engines may assess it as a 'low-quality page', which could hurt your ranking in results.

Other Tips

To make your advert more Search Engine Optimised, you can also add the following:

- Images – if you include an image in your advert you can add Alt Tags (left click on the picture and select Alt Text). Here you can type as many variations of descriptive keywords as you like. Readers will not be able to see them, but they will still be picked up by search engines.
- Hyperlinks – add hyperlinks to other relevant pages on your website.
- Share all your posts on social media – Twitter, Facebook, LinkedIn – for maximum impact.

CANDIDATE REGISTRATION

Candidate Assessment

Once you've generated candidate interest through your strategy, the next thing you need to do is assess the respondent's suitability. Is this candidate right for the job advert they have responded to? If not, can you place them elsewhere? Are they suitable for another registered vacancy, or for marketing into the sector more widely? My agency places 50 per cent of candidates in jobs we're actively recruiting for and the other half we market into companies because of the suitability of that candidate. We assess our candidates through an interview process – either on the phone or face-to-face. Remember, the interview is all about the person – you're dealing with people, not paper. The purpose of the interview is to assess:

- The candidate's suitability for a particular role, or
- How suitable they are for roles that might become available

- Their strengths and weaknesses
- How motivated they are to leave their current employment, and
- To obtain enough personal and professional information to market them.

A good recruiter will try to inspire loyalty and commitment from a candidate. The interview is an opportunity to *consult* with them and find the answer to the question, '*How can we help you take the next step in your career?*'

"The Limitless Recruiter favours the face-to-face interview because you learn so much more about a candidate when you can see the whites of their eyes." – James Kingston

---

Key Components of the Candidate Interview

Introduction

This is to put them at their ease and explain the process of the interview or call, and its purpose.

Obtaining personal information

This includes qualifications, contact details, IT knowledge, driving abilities, criminal convictions and any health issues. We ask for these details first because they are a good way to get the candidate chatting without having to open up too much.

Going through employment history

Again, this is fairly neutral but important information. Their employment history will tell you a lot about their levels of achievement and ambition. You need to drill down a bit here.

As well as noting the dates, job title and employer, get them to explain their key duties and responsibilities, and to talk about their biggest achievements and their strengths. A lot of candidates won't mention these unless asked specifically, but details like awards and accolades can really add value to a candidate's CV.

"The candidate interview is dealing with people, not paper." –
James Kingston

Current situation and aspirations – motivators, what they want from job

This is the crux of the interview process. Here, you want them to open up and explain to you why they want to leave their current employment – if they are employed – and what they are looking for in their next position. Here is a list of the topics you should cover in this part of the conversation:

- Their **current situation**, including their reasons for leaving, their level of motivation to move and how long they've been looking
- Their **personal motivators**, including reasons other than financial; their strengths; areas they would like to develop in; and their career aims
- Their **career requirements** – what is their ideal position and company? Would they take a salary cut to get what they want? Who wouldn't they work for? How far will they travel? Prompt them to prioritise their requirements.

THE ART OF RECRUITMENT

Tell them about your agency, how you work and what you do
This is where you sell yourself, your company and the service you can offer them. The reasons why they shouldn't use anyone else.

Agree an Action Plan
A vitally important but often neglected part of the interview or call. Just as on a client visit, you need to secure the candidate's commitment to let you represent them, preferably exclusively, especially if they are a strong candidate whom you are going to be able to place relatively easily. Make sure you get the candidate locked in. The first thing you ask is, *'Are you happy for us to send your CV to this client? Can you sign to confirm we're the first agency that has done that?'* This protects your interests.

Unless you're working on a retained assignment, as a Limitless Recruiter you shouldn't be sending the candidate's details to just one job. You should be marketing them out to suitable positions elsewhere too. If you don't, your competitors will. So agree an action plan: *'I'll send your CV to these ten companies over the next two weeks, and hopefully agree 3–5 interviews. Are you happy to work with us exclusively?'* Tell them why. *'The advantage is we get to talk to every single company on your behalf.'* The benefit is – *'You're not being presented in different ways by different agencies, which can lower the value of your CV. We'll make sure we agree the right way to present you and then do it professionally.'* If someone's gainfully employed, they don't want to be sent here, there and everywhere for interviews, which also increases the chance of their current employer finding out. They might also want to take an afternoon off to do three in a row. That's much easier to organise that if only one agency is involved and coordinating – *'This is better than five versions of your CV landing on someone's desk.'*

Generally, the key things that you are considering during the interview are: *How motivated are they to leave their job? What's the real reason? What might they jump at?*

Why are they looking for a job? If they've just been made redundant then their motivation to find a new one is going to be high and they're likely to be flexible about the kind of job they go for. If they're just dipping a toe in the market, get them to rank their motivators – from 1 to 10. You can't afford to waste time on candidates who are going to dither, any more than you can on clients who aren't going to follow through.

One of the first things you need to know is whether there's anything their current employer might do to keep the candidate, should they be offered a job elsewhere: would a small counter-offer be enough to persuade them to stay put? You need to keep checking this during the process, because sometimes the candidate's motivators might change between the day they come in to see you for registration and the date of a second interview you've arranged for them with an important client. Again, remember that it's all about people, not paper.

A surprising number of candidates will consider taking a cut in salary if the other conditions of employment suit them. This might be to achieve a better work-life balance. Here's a not uncommon example. A male candidate who was travelling 20 hours a week to his current employer was desperate to work closer to home. His relationship was under tremendous strain because he was never home in time to help with the children's bedtime. I found him a job only three miles away from his house. The new job wasn't easy and he had to take a 15 per cent pay cut, but he was really committed to it. He also got to see his family more in the mornings and evenings. The company were very happy with his performance and his marriage soon got back on track.

Another candidate worked on a building site in a physically demanding role, but his knees were starting to give out. We found him an office job that allowed him to use his experience in the industry, but without the physical strain. He's learning new skills and stepping up the corporate ladder now. The key takeaway here is that *it's not always financial reasons which motivate people to look for a new position*. As a consultant you sometimes have to be prepared to think outside the box to find a solution to the candidate's requirements.

Sometimes candidates don't consciously know what they want or what is motivating them. This is when you need to be the interrogator. Get a grasp of their character to find out what their motivators are and what they're good at. Ask them open questions like, *'Tell me what you like and don't like about your current job?'* This will often give you a clue as to where their motivation lies. They might dislike the boss, or the working hours. *'Tell me what you care about. If you had to prioritise package, role, location, career prospects and work/life balance from 1 to 5 – how would you do it?'* Flip it back to them – *'If I found you a job with good career prospects on your doorstep, but paying £5k less, would you take it?'* 'No.' *OK, so money is an important consideration.*

The candidate may not realise what their strengths are, but you need to find out in order to market them to clients. *'If I lined you up with five other people in your company, what makes you stand out? What are your key achievements to date? Can you think of a time when you've demonstrated these key values that my client is looking for?'* If it is a specific job that you're interviewing them for, don't be afraid to ask, *'What makes you think you could do this role successfully?'* After all, they're bound to be asked that question should they get an interview!

Remember 'MSC'. What *Must* this job have? What *Should* it have? What *Could* it have? Then flip it again – *'If this job had A, B, and C; but not X, Y and Z – would that be acceptable?'* Find out the candidate's red lines for taking, or turning down, a job.

This is another stage where the Limitless Recruiter will distinguish themselves. Many consultants glide through the candidate interview on autopilot, but the Limitless Recruiter will drill down, dig and find out the vital bits of information that make the whole process so much easier and more rewarding – for the candidate, the client and the consultant.

The whole point of candidate interviews is to find out everything you can about the candidate – what makes them tick and, ultimately, what job they want and what job they will take. At its best it's a process of discovery for both parties – the skilled consultant will make the candidate think about their situation and the possibilities open to them in ways they hadn't before. More bluntly, as a recruiter you need to know if the candidate will take the job, if offered. Especially when good candidates are scarce!

The Limitless Recruiter will

• Ask a strong candidate to name five to ten companies they would love to work for. This immediately gives you an 'in' with those companies. *'I've just met JB. He loves your company and has always wanted to work there. Can I just tell you some of his key achievements?'* You can also take the reverse approach and ask them which companies they don't want to work for, and why. This is useful information for marketing the candidate, but it might also reconfirm what you've heard about particular organisations – that they don't pay on time, or treat their staff badly, for instance.

• Notice body language. It's obvious really, or it should be, but a face-to-face interview will tell you things that a telephone interview simply can't. Body language, confidence and presentation can be assessed, and advice given when necessary.

TAKING REFERENCES

Once you've concluded the interview, you need to take references. Don't delay with this. There is nothing worse than putting a candidate forward to a client and then finding you can't find a single former employer with a good word to say about them. Plus, a good reference is one of the strongest marketing tools. Think how often you buy things on the recommendation of others – word-of-mouth or online reviews, for instance. A glowing reference from a candidate's previous boss not only puts your mind at rest about the candidate's qualities, but will also substantiate any claims you make on their behalf in a candidate profile. Some people are nervous about asking for a reference prior to an offer being made. Sometimes where there is only one previous current employer you may have to wait. But this is to protect you, your valuable time and your reputation, so what is worse? In order to overcome a candidate's nervousness about being referenced early, say *'Clients put the CVs we send them to the top of their list because of our attention to detail. It's why they prefer to use us over other agencies and the benefit to you means they are more likely to want to see you before any other candidate.'* Passive candidates are harder to persuade, as they aren't actively looking, so asking for the name of a former colleague, client or business associate who could give a recommendation might be a better tactic.

Why do We Take References?
• To validate candidate's skills, experience and personality
• As part of a quality pre-screening process
• It enables you to promote the candidate better.

Benefits of Taking References
• Increases your matching ability
• Gives the client peace of mind
• Gives you peace of mind
• It reduces the time spent on inferior candidates – people you won't be able to place
• Lessens the chance of rebates on placement fees

• An opportunity to introduce you and your agency to potential clients.

'Remember, like any other call, taking a reference is an opportunity to develop a new business relationship.' – James Kingston

---

Here are the essential areas you should cover when taking a reference:

Introduction
• You and your agency
• What you are hoping to achieve with the reference, and why.

Employment Overview
• How long was the applicant employed?
• When did they start?
• When did they leave?
• Why did they leave?
• What was their attendance record like?
• What was their position?
• What were their specific responsibilities and duties?
• Who did they report to?
• Who reported to them?
• Were any disciplinary actions taken against them?

'When asking the client's opinions about a candidate's strengths and weaknesses, emphasise that their answers can be 'on or off the record' to encourage them to open up more.'

Personal Overview

• How would you (the client) describe them?
• What are their strengths?
• What are their areas of development?
• How do they relate to others?
• How do they perform in a team?
• What is their potential?
• What is their management style or personality like?
• Work ethic – are they honest, reliable and hardworking?
• What are their communication skills like?
• How do they perform under pressure?
• Are they commercially-minded?
• What is their technical ability?
• Do they have a good eye for detail?

Strengths

• How does this person rank in a list of similar staff you've employed, and why?
• What did they do well for you?
• Would you recommend them for the role they have applied for? Describe the job without giving away the company details, unless they already know. If the answer is *'Yes, I would'*, ask if you can

tell that to the client you are recruiting for.
- Would you re-employ them?

Weaknesses
- If the reference is not very good, drill down into why they didn't work out – it could just be that they were the wrong person for that job, but that means that another position might suit them better.
- Remember, the employer may have their own motivations for giving a good or bad reference, e.g. covering up for their own deficiencies, or wanting to see a weak candidate employed by a competitor! It doesn't happen often, but always be open to all possibilities.

Your Chance to Shine
- How did you recruit this candidate? How do you normally recruit? Are you recruiting now? What is your current situation? Could my details be of use to you, or who can I speak to who recruits?
- Promote your agency!

Reference-taking Checklist:
- Did you obtain a good reference?
- Did you convert the employer to a client? Take a vacancy? Arrange a client visit?

Reference-taking Tips
- Keep the questions as open as possible – avoid simple 'yes'/'no' answers where possible – and let the employer do the talking.

• Don't ask leading questions. Instead of, *'JB said that his key duties included...'*, ask, *'What were JB's key duties?'*

CV WRITING AND CANDIDATE PROFILING
Writing a good CV is a key skill for any consultant. In old-school recruitment, candidates were often just presented over the phone. This may still be the case for some freelance recruitment roles, but for senior positions, today's clients invariably want a detailed CV. Every agency will have their own preferred format for CV writing so I'll just provide some pointers that should help you go the extra mile.

Candidate Profile
Begin with the candidate profile. A profile is shorter than a CV but it provides a succinct and persuasive snapshot of the candidate, ideally tailored to match the vacancy that you are submitting them for. This can be incorporated in, or attached to, the CV before you send it to the client. If you've done your job at the interview stage, and taken references, then you should have all the information that you need to write their profile and market them to the client. You're selling the person here, as well as their employment history. Sometimes candidates don't do a very good job of selling themselves, so this profile can be crucial. These are some of the things you should feature in the profile:

• *The candidate's USPs* – what impressed you about the candidate and how they presented themselves to you
• *Their key achievements* – particularly the ones relevant to the vacancy at hand

- *Their career aspirations* – and how those match with the vacancy they are being put forward for
- *Their attributes according to former employers* – a standout quote from a good reference is always useful here
- *Their desired renumeration* – clients expect this information to be included. If there is a mismatch with the package on offer, make it clear whether the candidate might consider other benefits as part of a deal
- *Availability* – this may be an important consideration for the client, especially if there is an important project in the offing
- *Summarise* – briefly recap why you are recommending the candidate.

CV Writing

The candidate's CV is arguably the most important element of any job application. While most candidates are hopefully good at their jobs, they're often not so good at presenting themselves favourably in their CVs. Writing a CV is not something that most of them do very often, whereas a recruitment consultant will write hundreds in their career. You need to take the raw material they present you with and shape it into a work of art.

As I said earlier, every agency will have their own template for CV writing. We try to keep our CVs to a maximum three pages in length, preferably two pages, but occasionally a candidate's relevant information is so important that you need to make room for it.

The first page should provide basic information about a

candidate – their current role, location, notice period, salary – as well as the candidate profile, if this is not attached separately. The idea is to give the client a snapshot of the candidate, but also catch their interest to look deeper for more detail about them. Legibility and layout are key. You need to be continually giving the client reasons to keep reading through until they make the decision to call or email you to arrange an interview.

CV Writing – Tips and Tricks

- *Think of the CV as an advertisement* designed to attract attention and spark interest in the product, which in this instance is your candidate. You still need to convert that interest into a sale – or in this case an interview and hopefully a job offer – but it's the CV that places your candidate into one of three piles on a hirer's desk: 'Must interview', 'Maybe', and 'No'. Follow these tips to make sure your candidate becomes a 'Must interview'.
- *Start with a summary*. Recruiters spend an average of only 20 seconds reviewing a resume, so put your best foot forward. Start with a 100-word summary of your candidate's experience, results and qualifications. The best CVs are easy on the eye and highlight the key information needed to impress the client.
- *Play to your candidate's strengths.* Shape the structure of the CV to reflect the candidate's career to date in the best light. This is particularly important if you're sending a CV on spec, rather than for a specific vacancy, because you can't be certain what might tip the balance and get the client's interest. If she has years of relevant experience, lead with that. List her positions,

starting with the most recent, and end with her qualifications. But if your candidate is a graduate, then open with his academic achievements and the quality of training he has received. Highlight their key achievements in each role. If they've got a particular qualification that few achieve, or if they've won a professional award, highlight that on the front page in bold (as long as it's relevant to the job you're submitting them for).

- *Less is more.* Ideally the CV should fill no more than two sides of A4 – three if you have a lot of positions to cover. This isn't the time to go into everything in detail, that's what an interview is for. Spend more time focusing on things that relate directly to the position you're putting the candidate forward for, because that's what a recruiter is interested in. Which leads to …

- *Tailoring the CV to the vacancy.* Pick out the key requirements from the vacancy spec, then address each of them on the CV. Instead of including every good quality or achievement, the CV will be far stronger if you cherry-pick experiences that your client can see will benefit their business. Include specific projects, dates and results for maximum effect.

- *Writing in plain English.* Avoid jargon and corporate buzzwords. A lot of people use this kind of language because they lack confidence in their written skills. There's no need to tie yourself in knots trying to sell a candidate. Just use simple, direct expressions that are instantly understandable and clearly explain the candidate's suitability for the role. Make sure the CV is written in the 'third person' – *'Jane is an outstanding blacksmith…'* – and not the original 'first person' in the CV you received from the candidate.

- *Professional presentation.* Present the CV as you'd like your candidate to appear at an interview – clean and professional. Use a single, legible font (and stick to one), and don't be tempted by quirky design elements which might attract attention for all the wrong reasons. Avoid confusing layouts – condense long paragraphs into bullet points and don't allow page breaks to interrupt mid-flow. Instead of jumping from point to point, present your candidate's career in reverse chronological order, with clear sections for their employment history and academic qualifications. Don't give a client any reason to stop reading about your candidate. And **Comic Sans?** Just no.
- *Check It!* When you think you've finished the CV, read it again. Preferably aloud. Even better, get someone else to read it. Take the time to fix every typo, grammatical error or confusing phrase. There's simply no excuse for spelling mistakes or bad grammar in such an important document.

THE LIMITLESS RECRUITER WILL…
- **Be generating both active and passive candidates**
- **When recruiting for a vacancy, ask the client where they found their last candidate**
- **Maintain lists of the 20 best candidates in key roles – and keep in touch with them**
- **Have an 'aftercare strategy' for previously-placed candidates. That way, you'll know when they're next looking for a new challenge**

- Be aware of what SEO is and have a basic understanding of how it works
- Favour the face-to-face interview over the telephone call – you learn so much more about the candidate
- Agree an Action Plan with candidates that involves marketing them for more than one job
- Drill down for the candidate's real motivators
- Ask a strong candidate to name the 5–10 companies they would love to work for – then market them in to them
- Remember that taking a reference is an opportunity to develop a new business relationship
- Keep CVs short and devoid of jargon, and make sure they play to a candidate's strengths
- Never use Comic Sans!

Chapter Five: The Client

"Selling is only directed at people. You can't make a sale unless it is to another person." – Richard Denny

- Market Research
- Strategic Account Management
- Sales Calls
- The Client Visit
- Vacancy Registration
- Retainers

How you select and manage your client relationships will determine how successful you are in your career. I cannot overstate the importance of doing the groundwork to ensure you have a good portfolio of clients at different levels of development, and that this portfolio should have objectives which are constantly reviewed and renewed. To start with, you need to do some Market Research – to ensure you have the best, most comprehensive list of businesses in your sector to refine. Then, by applying Strategic Account Management (SAM), you can hone your list of potential customers into clients and start developing business relationships – through regular mailshots, sales calls and client visits. This will lead to recruitment opportunities to register vacancies from them and you'll be on your way to making placements in no time. You are aiming to build partnerships in recruitment with your clients – that is the ideal.

THE ART OF RECRUITMENT

MARKET RESEARCH

In essence, Market Research is the planning needed prior to a sales call. This involves getting to know your market and finding the decision-makers, and then planning who you're going to talk to – and how. All before you pick up the phone. Like every aspect of recruitment, Market Research should be ongoing, never static. Companies change, sectors change, the wider economy changes. If you don't take note and keep updating your knowledge of the market-place, you'll soon be left behind by more on-the-ball competitors.

In its broadest definition, Market Research is used to determine the viability of a potential area of development. As I mentioned in an earlier chapter, when we are considering moving into a new sector, we check out how big the opportunity is: crudely, how many clients are in that sector. We need to determine whether the number of potential clients in an area will be enough to sustain a team of consultants.

Then, looking more closely at individual companies, we need to determine whether they're hiring and if so, how often. We need to understand how each company functions. We find out who the Decision-Makers (DMs) are. There are many ways to do this, including searching the Internet, professional networking channels and even a company's own website. Not to mention the old-fashioned method of picking up the phone and asking. You'd be surprised how quickly a well-structured fact-finding call can obtain all the key info and contacts in a company. We can do follow-up calls with candidates who have been placed with the company and ask them about current vacancies, and who the best people are to speak to about recruitment. Colleagues are often an invaluable source, too. It's amazing how much neglected information is available in your own office.

Market Research also embraces knowing everything about the roles in the sector you're going to be recruiting for. When you speak to a decision-maker, if you can demonstrate that you know what they do and what they're responsible for, you'll create an instant bond of empathy when it comes to discussing their recruitment needs. You'll also be aware of what they're *not* responsible for. There's no quicker way to alienate a potential client than by presenting a candidate – no matter how accomplished – who doesn't fall into the categories of staff that person would hire.

Every consultant who comes to work for me has to do a presentation on their account base for the sector they're working on. In order to sell these companies to a candidate, you need to know them inside out. I always say to the consultant, *'Tell me five facts about that company. For instance, what's the turnover? How many offices do they have? Who's their best client? How do they make their money? What are their Unique Selling Points (USPs) to potential candidates? What are the company structure and the key positions and the name of each person and, equally important, who are their key competitors?'*

When I first went into recruitment, none of this training was available to me. In fact, as part of the interview process with my first agency, I was given a phone and told to obtain five internal contact lists, speak to fifty decision-makers and get two vacancies by any means possible by the end of the day. I had no idea what I was meant to say or do. Thankfully I've always been able to wing it, but it was hardly the best way to start. Knowing what I know now, I would have done so much more planning to increase my chances of success. This is what Market Research is for – not only to give you confidence before you make a sales call to a client or a candidate, but so that you're spending your most valuable commodity (time) on the right people and with the right purpose.

To recap, before you start to consider approaching clients you need to know everything about the sector you are recruiting in. You need to be aware of all the clients – existing and potential – in the area or region that you are planning to service. This is achieved through Market Research.

In the first three months of starting on a new desk, or opening up a new sector, you need to identify every single client in your market. This is not as straightforward or obvious as it sounds. I've had consultants working for me who had been in recruitment for 20 years and they didn't know every business on their patch. They'd relied on the company database of clients and then suddenly discovered that a company with a £50 million turnover just down the road was recruiting. Situations change all the time and you need to be able to change with them. This is especially true if you are recruiting UK-wide, or globally, rather than in a smaller, defined area where it's potentially easier to keep on top of things.

Identifying Potential Clients

Always be looking to add more businesses to your client list – ones that you don't know about yet. They are where your potential growth lies. How do you find this information? There is a myriad of ways. First, yes, look at your current database – the office's master account list, if there is one. (If there isn't, ask if you can set one up: it'll save everyone a lot of time and confusion.) Do you notice any omissions or out-of-date details? Ask around the office. They might have recently come back from a company visit where a client mentioned they're opening a new branch in the region. Update the list.

Now look at the companies. Go onto their websites. What accreditations do they have? What awards have they won? If you then go onto the accreditations and awards websites, they'll probably have a list of many other businesses in the same sector. Check that they're all on your list, and if they're not, check whether they have a presence in your area. If the awards mention high-achieving individuals, there's potential right there for head-hunting. It's the same whether you're looking for hairdressers or quantity surveyors. Every industry has its accreditations and awards bodies.

Media Sources and Advertised Vacancies

Every industry also has its own dedicated media publications. Each year, some of these newspapers, magazines, journals and websites will publish a list of the top 50 or 100 companies in that sector. It's a ready-made shopping list for the wily consultant. For small to medium enterprises (SMEs) you may need to look at more regional and local media for similar details. Use your imagination. There are always outlets to be discovered which will lead you to the information you are seeking.

Or take another approach. Think of the top five positions you will be recruiting for in the sector. Then type them into Google, or job boards like uk.indeed.com, with a regional locator. Filter the results by 'employers only'. You'll find companies advertising roles that you wouldn't learn about any other way.

On company websites, go to their vacancies page. You can set up an alert to inform you when the page is updated by using a change detection service like watchthatpage.com. That way you'll be the first to know of any vacancies being advertised by those companies. This is a great way to generate leads for the lead calls we'll come on to talk about. Also, look at the websites of competitor agencies – what clients do they say they work with? What testimonials do they have? Leave no stone unturned to build up your list.

CV Stripping

Another great way of building up a potential client list is by stripping candidates' CVs of previous companies they have worked for. Pull together a hundred CVs of candidates in key positions in your region and note every company named on those CVs. Some may have gone into administration and some may be irrelevant, but I guarantee you'll come away with companies to call that you'd never have heard of or found out about by any other means.

The Internet

In a world where everyone wants to be on the first page of Google, Search Engine Optimisation (SEO – see Chapter 4) is getting so good that typing in a business category in an area or region – software engineers in Birmingham, for instance – will produce plenty of potential new clients to contact. Beware, though: sometimes you can turn up too many and you'll lose focus. Try to be specific about the area.

So, now what do we do with all this new information? That's where Strategic Account Management comes in.

STRATEGIC ACCOUNT MANAGEMENT

Account Selection

Right, so now you've got your list. It's daunting, but this is where it gets interesting. Before you start making calls you need to decide who, from that list, you're going to call.

When I entered recruitment, I was given the leftover accounts and contacts that no other consultant wanted. It's often the way. I had a list of companies and did what any trainee consultant was meant to do back then – pick up the phone and start calling them all, one by one. I had a process in my head: I was going to identify the key decision-makers. I would then keep in touch with them regularly and eventually I would pick up a vacancy. I created what I call an MTV cycle – Mailer, Telephone call, Visit. Every contact would get 3–4 emails, 3–4 phone calls and a visit every three months.

One of those companies was a small company with a £10 million turnover, which is why it had been largely ignored by the rest of the team. (They were more interested in big, blue-chip corporations – the glamour accounts.) So I picked up this small construction company account. They started winning lots of lucrative contracts and grew to become the largest contractor in the South West region, with a turnover of over £200 million, before being bought out by Balfour Beatty. Within twelve months of my picking up the phone to them, they became our office's biggest account. It just goes to show that you should never pre-judge or write off an account. *You need to keep checking in with the clients.*

However, you do need to be selective. An account worth working on is one where you could potentially make multiple placements a year, not a one-man band that might employ a single contractor for a day. Though one placement a year with 20 clients, if your average fee is £25,000, is no bad thing. You just need to be thinking about where all your placements are going to come from and how much potential spend each client can offer.

Look at it from another angle. You've got your spreadsheet. On an annual basis, if I'm going to aim to make 20, 50 or 100 placements, where are they all going to come from? If you want to be a Limitless Recruiter, a million-pound biller, and your average fee is going to be £5,000, then you need to be making 200 placements.

The optimum number of accounts to work on is between 30 and 40 over a three-month period – once you've established the potential of those accounts. These are the companies you'll be networking and contacting regularly to establish a relationship.

Grade Your Portfolio

So whether you're just starting out, taking over a desk or just wanting to add value to what you do, the first thing you need to do is call everyone. Then, over the first three months, grade your portfolio of accounts into the four categories explained below:

Key Accounts

A good recruitment consultant should have 60 per cent of their work in Key Accounts. These are the hot clients that you have recruitment activity with on a regular basis, such as placements, interviews and live vacancies, and where you have good relationships with the key decision-makers.

Rising Stars

25% of your accounts should be Rising Stars – this could be an established client opening a new office in your area, or a new client winning a lot of business – basically, it's a future Key Account.

Status Clients

Finally, there are the 'Status' clients. Historically, they've been good clients but now they're not in the market. Perhaps you did a massive amount of recruitment for them last year and so they're quite settled at the present time. But recruitment is cyclical, so the need may arise again next year. You should spend no more than 5% of your time on these clients.

If you're aiming to work on 40 accounts that means you'll need 24 Key Accounts, 10 Rising Stars, 4 Status and 2 Streamline Accounts.

Streamline Accounts

The accounts that aren't particularly attractive and don't spend much money are what we call the 'Streamline' customers. It might be a very good organisation that currently doesn't have a good name, is known for treating its staff badly, or has terrible paying terms and a Preferred Supplier List of twenty companies. You can't afford to ignore them, in case a new broom comes in and changes everything around, but you don't want to be spending much time – no more than 10% – on them either.

Client Categories

Now you've got your business development list and you've graded it. The next thing you need to do is map out each of the companies on your list. You need to build an organigram (diagram of personnel) showing the structure of each company. You don't need to know who every single person is, just the four types of employee you'll be hoping to establish good working relationships with. These are the Gatekeepers, Influencers, Approvers and Decision-Makers. Please note that it's not just the Decision-Makers!

Decision-Maker (DM)

These are the key people who can initiate business relationships and who are closely involved in the day-to-day recruitment process. Managing Directors, Heads of Department and Human Resources (HR) fit into this category.

Approver

Not as directly involved in recruitment as the DM, but has the ability to block recommendations from them. A Finance Director or board member, for example.

Influencer

Does not get involved in allocating new business but can influence the recruitment process for better or worse. For instance, you may know a Managing Director who does not deal with the day-to-day recruitment of low-level staff. But her internal recommendation could persuade the HR department to start using your agency and put you on a Preferred Supplier List.

Gatekeeper

Can hinder a relationship with the DM by blocking access or withholding information. Receptionists and PAs are examples. They can't give you a 'yes' or a 'no', but they might give you access to the DM's diary, give you their phone number, or tell you if they're hiring. I always make an effort to get to know every PA of every client I deal with on a first-name basis. They hold all the keys. It's really worth cultivating a great relationship with these people and having them on your side can be invaluable.

They're called 'Gatekeepers' because they hold the keys to the gate you have to get past. Although you wouldn't think it, these innocuous employees can be the biggest barrier to establishing good business relationships with clients – if you approach them in the wrong way.

THE ART OF RECRUITMENT

Gatekeepers come in different guises and there are generally two different reasons for getting past them: firstly to get through to a client, and secondly to head-hunt a candidate.

Remember, a Gatekeeper can be anyone who picks ups the phone – a colleague in an open-plan office for instance – not just a receptionist. So you need to be able to be discreet, when necessary. If you're head-hunting and you introduce yourself as *'Mark from Head-Hunting Recruitment'*, you might embarrass the candidate or get them into trouble. The person taking the call might shout out who you are across the office. The candidate is certainly not going to be well-disposed to speaking to you after that.

In this situation I use a pseudonym – made up of the first name of my old boss and the name of the street I worked in – but do what works for you. I'd always stress, *'He'll know what it's regarding'* or *'I'm returning his call'*.

If it's a sales call, the first priority is to show the Gatekeeper respect – they're only doing their job after all. They have probably been instructed to screen calls, to avoid their boss being bombarded with unsolicited approaches from agencies and other organisations. You need to get them onside, rather than get their back up.

The key to doing this is to learn their name, then build up a rapport – introduce some humour into the conversation. Tell them why you're calling. In the first ten seconds, try to establish some easy common ground – make a joke. Try to catch their name, so you can use it next time: *'Hi Lyn, it's James from KB here – yes, we spoke the other day.'* It takes a barrier down. Receptionists get more sales calls than anyone in any position, so there tend to be a lot of barriers up.

When you've made your request you can preclude any further conversation by saying *'thank you.'* 'Thank you' is a great way of telling someone to do what you want, if said with the correct mix of authority and warmth.

'Hello, it's J from KB – can you put me through to John H – thank you.' The *'thank you,'* will shut down any further conversation – it's a good way to try to get through to the client politely.

Listen and gauge the person. You should be able to get a strong idea of their personality type in the first ten to twenty seconds. If they're a cold fish and repeated attempts to warm them up yield no result, try calling outside office hours – 8 am, lunchtime, at the end of the day – when someone else will likely pick up the phone. Generally, though, as they'll usually be the first point of contact, you want to build up a rapport.

I love Gatekeepers. I buy them gifts and make time to talk to them when I go on a visit. I learn their names. I get to know about their family and where they like to go on holiday. British people can't get enough of talking about holidays and the weather – anything not related to work. Build up that knowledge so that when you call back you can ask them about their life – people naturally open up and talk about themselves when prompted.

You're aiming to set yourself aside from the crowd. Then you can ask for more. If you're purely transactional, asking perfunctory questions without much enthusiasm, then you might occasionally get an email address, or get put through, but you'll never develop the trust and empathy that will work in your favour.

If you're a Limitless Recruiter, then you'll see the Gatekeeper as the person who can help you get what you want and need, and therefore as someone deserving of your time, attention and respect. You'll aspire to build up a stronger relationship with them than almost anyone else in the company. They can give you the keys to the kingdom. They can help or hinder you more than anyone else.

I have great relationships with Gatekeepers – they will give me mobile numbers, introduce me to other key personnel in their companies, even book me appointments with their boss without my having to speak to the boss directly.

Goal: find out five non-work-related facts about each Gatekeeper – whether they are a man or a woman, find out their names, where they go on holiday, what family they have, any spare-time hobbies and interests, how they get to work.

Empathise with them – *'You must get hundreds of calls from agencies?'*

'Yes, I do.'

'What's the most annoying call you've had?'

'Well, there's someone who won't take 'no' for an answer – he rings every day and my boss does not want to talk to him.'

'If I promise not to do that, will you put me through to John?'

Tell them why you're calling, *'I'm trying to get a job for a young man who's just been made redundant. He's been with his employer for five years and he's got a young family and he's really keen to work for your company.'* I did this with the Gatekeeper of a small company in Devon and she was the one who ended up persuading her boss to take my candidate on. The power of the Gatekeeper should never be under-estimated!

It won't always work. If you've tried everything and you're making no headway, to the point where you suspect you're being regarded as a nuisance, then be prepared to give the company to a colleague for a try – a different name and a different approach might work. Sometimes a particular voice or accent will grate. We've all reacted irrationally in that way. But try to be honest and build up a relationship of mutual respect. I know consultants who have called the same Gatekeeper using a different name each time, and pretending to be from a different company, but people aren't stupid – they might recognise the voice, or that the same ID number is coming up on their switchboard. Patience, empathy and respect will get you what you want nine times out of ten. Use them, don't abuse them.

Scale Relationships

Now scale each of the relationships from 1 to 5, with 5 being the strongest. If each consultant does this and the information is accessible on a master office spreadsheet then, in an instant, any consultant will be able to see who knows the key category personnel in each company and the strength of an existing relationship. For instance, one of my consultants could come to me and say, *'I've got a really strong candidate to market to Joe Bloggs Finance and I noticed you've scored your relationship with the MD as 4 out of 5. Is there anything you can tell me to help me get through to him?'* It takes the second-guessing out of the situation, as long as everyone keeps the spreadsheet updated.

THE ART OF RECRUITMENT

Mailers

We'll look at the content of Sales Calls and Client Visits in more detail in this chapter. But here, just a quick word about Mailers. These days, it's most likely to be an email rather than a letter that you send by post, though due to the volume of emails we all receive now, the latter can still be really effective. We did a gift exercise to 250 decision-makers, with a hard copy salary survey and covering letter, received 20 exclusive vacancies from it and secured one retainer in the process.

'Ring, don't Ping!' is my slogan. A phone call is always more effective than an email, but we live in a busy world and there are times when a mailer can really hit the spot. For instance, there's no denying that you can reach many clients in an instant with a great mailer, whereas it might take you a day to speak to them all personally.

Imagine that you've got a great candidate who's just come on the market. He's on a job board and every agency and their dog is chasing him. You're up against it. What do you do? Firstly, you identify all the clients who might be seriously interested in this candidate, make sure you have their current email addresses. Then you create a mouth-watering, exciting teaser email. Not too long – short enough to get the attention and just long enough to cover the essentials. You need to get this candidate in front of your clients before anyone else does, with all the usual caveats about General Data Protection Regulation and candidate permissions.

You need to create something that is going to make them come straight back to you. Imagine the candidate has ten years' experience in a key industry role and is now keen to move on. If you send him in a mailshot to fifty of his company's competitors, if they are in the market for someone with that experience you will hear from them almost immediately. There's the benefit of a candidate mailer, in a nutshell. As part of a wider strategy, including sales calls and client visits, it definitely adds something extra to the portfolio of the Limitless Recruiter. It should be used sparingly, though. A candidate mailer should go out no more than once a fortnight, or possibly weekly if you work on a large, fast-moving market.

Other reasons for sending a mailer might include an introduction to your services, if you're unable to get through to the client on the phone. Or a link to a topical blog about an industry topic – a salary survey, for instance. Make sure it's something that the client might be interested in. It sounds obvious, but DON'T send speculative CVs two or three times a week – it's the best way to get the client to close the door on you, or filter your messages to a junk folder.

Tips for Writing a Great Mailer
- Make sure the Subject Line is specific and relevant – and short. Between two and six words is optimum
- WIIFM – 'What's In It For Me?' Imagine reading it from the client's point of view. Every word must be relevant and make them want to read on
- Make sure it contains a call to action, even if this is as simple as asking them to contact you for further details.

Implementing Strategic Account Management
In summary, this is the activity cycle you need to follow:

1. By the End of Month One
- Identify 30–40 companies to develop. What does your portfolio look like? Sort them into Key Accounts, Rising Stars, Status and Streamline Clients. Make sure they are in the right proportion
- Have an overview of all the accounts (e.g. five facts/USPs)
- Complete an organigram for each company – identifying key client categories and scaling relationships
- Have completed an initial MTV cycle, to be repeated until the end of month three.

2. By the End of Month Six – Review and Repeat
- Review accounts – activity, placements, interviews, vacancies, visits, calls, networking
- New account selection
- Repeat MTV cycle.

Review
It's the easiest thing to neglect, but it's very important to keep reviewing the accounts and introducing new clients into the process, or else your activity will become stale. Also, some accounts and relationships take longer than a few phone calls to develop. As long as you are getting some positive response it's worth repeating the cycle with the same account for another three months. But sometimes a new face can make all the difference. So

we change our accounts around every 3–6 months to freshen things up and give other consultants the chance to warm up a relationship that's gone cold. If you let people sit on what they view as a dud account and not do anything with it, you might be missing out on a potential gold-mine. By faithfully implementing the MTV cycle, if the opportunity is there you should have the chance to discover it.

SALES CALLS

How many times do you hear people saying, after making a phone call, *'Oh, I wish I'd asked that'* or *'I forgot to tell them about...'* It's not a big deal if you're phoning a friend about lunch – you can just ring them back again. But with a sales call it indicates a failure to prepare properly. It's also not so easy to keep phoning back without irritating the person you're calling.

Before a good consultant picks up the phone to speak to a client they should be thinking, 'MUST, SHOULD, COULD' (MSC). *What MUST I get from the call? What SHOULD I get from the call? What COULD I get from the call?* It's the planning required for a successful sales call.

Sales Call Preparation

Below are the seven stages that should constitute every successful sales call. The most important thing is that you have clearly defined objectives and a structure for the call in your mind *before* you phone a client:

i. PREPARATION (Must, Should, Could)

THE ART OF RECRUITMENT

ii. INTRODUCTION

iii. IDENTIFY NEED (questions about the individual, the company and their recruitment)

iv. SUMMARISE (show understanding)

v. OFFER SOLUTION (relevant USPs and benefits)

vi. ACTION/CLOSE

vii. FOLLOW UP.

i. PREPARATION

The worst-case scenario for any sales call should be that you come away from it with at least five new pieces of information. Let's say you're making a blank canvassing call, where you know little about the company you're phoning, and your purpose is to find out as much as you can. These might be the *'Must, Should, Could'* (MSC) in this scenario:

MUST – identify and speak to the decision-maker for the department relevant to your sector

SHOULD – market in a suitable candidate and ask the DM five questions about their business and their recruitment methods

COULD – get a commitment from the DM to see the candidate you think might be suitable, identify a potential vacancy, or arrange a company visit.

You see? Immediately, the call – indeed, any sales call you make – has a purpose and a measurable goal. Remember to make sure the goal is realistic, or you may end up alienating the client. Also, be flexible in the call. If the client's offices start to burn down during your conversation, they may not prioritise a company visit in the next week. Conversely, if it transpires that they have an urgent vacancy, be prepared to take a detailed job spec, know your T&Cs and line up some interview slots as soon as possible.

ii. INTRODUCTION

Think about how you're going to introduce yourself in the call. A great way to open a cold call is to tell them what you do and your USP to them. As an example,

'Hi, this is James from Kingston Barnes; we help building contractors recruit the best talent in construction. I noticed on your website you are advertising for a quantity surveyor vacancy. I may have a candidate who could fit the bill, could you tell me a bit more about the position?'

A question to get the client talking about their company is always good. Have several questions planned in advance – they might be prompted by something you've noticed on the client's website – a vacancy or a bit of company news. It might be something you've heard from a candidate or a colleague. Just make it engaging and inviting – something the client will enjoy talking about.

Try and avoid cringeworthy openers like, *I hope you're well? Apologies for the call…* I hate it when people apologise for calling! People are the most important part of any successful business, so great recruitment is vital to that success. Just don't be over-familiar. I receive sales calls all the time. Take it from me: it's very annoying to be called 'mate' or 'buddy' or 'darling' by someone you've never spoken to before.

THE ART OF RECRUITMENT

iii. IDENTIFY NEED

Next, you need to identify the client's needs. This is really important. What you are looking for are the reasons why the client will buy into what you can offer them. Questions about the individual, their company and their recruitment process are key. Check out my Top Questions to Ask a Client later on in this chapter, but here are some good questions you can use. Always have specific ones relevant to the client you are planning to contact:

- *How are you finding the market at present?*
- *How are you performing compared to previous years?*
- *What are your business plans over the next 6–12 months?*
- *What type of work is it that you do? What is a typical example?*
- *How many people do you employ?*
- *How long have you been at this company for?*
- *What was it that attracted you to the company? Or keeps you with them!*
- *What is it about your company that makes you better than your competitors?*
- *How do you think your company is perceived in the marketplace by potential employees?*
- *What's the business's biggest challenge?*
- *Who are your main competitors?*
- *How do you typically recruit? And who in the business does the recruiting?*
- *Have you recruited much in the past 12 months?*
- *Where do you get your work from?*
- *What type of people work for you?*

My favourite question is: *'Is there a particular type of person who – if they came on the market – you'd be interested in seeing?* This is a great enquiry because it gives you an idea of a future follow-up call to spec in a candidate, but it can also lead to a potential vacancy.

Keep the questions as open as possible, encouraging the client to speak freely. And use the other organ on the phone – your ears. Listening to what the person is actually saying and using that information to direct your questions and think about the solution is key. So many salespeople are so keen to just talk that they don't actually find out any needs or understand what the potential client is thinking. Check out my 'Top Questions to Ask a Client' later on in this chapter.

iv. SUMMARISE and

v. OFFER SOLUTION

Take notes as you talk, so you can summarise your conversation and then offer solutions based on your company's relevant USPs and benefits. The client is likely to be interested in your service if it saves them time, money or hassle – or preferably a combination of all these factors. So in your questioning, try and identify their most pressing needs and then highlight how you can provide the solution: *'Okay, so I appreciate you've had bad experiences in the past and you're feeling fed up with agencies not understanding your business and sending unsuitable candidates. Because we are experts in your field, we know what type of people would fit in with your business. Ultimately this will save you time finding the right person and you'll waste less energy meeting people who don't match your requirements.'*

vi. ACTION/CLOSE

This is also the point at which you should be securing agreement on a plan of action between you and the client: *'So, if I can get three suitable candidates' CVs to you next Tuesday, you'll be able to interview them on Friday. What times are you available that day, so that we can pencil them in now?'*

vii. FOLLOW UP

And finally, don't forget to agree a follow-up action: *'I'll call you tomorrow to make sure the CVs have arrived,'* or *'Okay, I appreciate you aren't looking for anyone at the moment. I will drop you an email now with my contact information so if anything changes you can call me. How does the 27th of next month sound for an update call? What time shall I pop in the diary?'*

Types of Sales Calls

There are many different types of sales call in recruitment, and even non-sales calls are usually an opportunity for business development. The Limitless Recruiter should be doing the following on a regular basis:

New Business Call – also known as the 'cold call', this is the call where you don't know much about the company, except what your initial market research has turned up. You might not know who the decision-makers are, or even whether they're looking for staff. Your sole purpose here is to promote your business. The company might be part of your development plan for a new sector – one of 40 companies you need to network, understand and build a relationship with. It's often perceived as the hardest call to make. Having said that, there's always the chance they are desperate to fill vacancies because their preferred suppliers have let them down. So keep an open mind and approach the call positively – with a growth mindset. Remember, you can only call someone for the first time once! The next call will be following up, filling in the blanks and looking for an opportunity for business.

Marketing Call – this usually involves marketing (or 'speccing', as we like to call it) a placeable candidate to a client. You don't know whether they will be interested – this is what you need to find out – so make sure your introduction is clear in purpose. Always tell them who you are, what you do and how that might be of benefit to them: *'Hi, it's James here from KB recruitment. We help contractors find the leading talent in construction and we are exclusively representing a candidate who has been working for your competitor for the past ten years in an operational capacity. He is keen to look for a new opportunity. You are a company he has always been interested in working for. Do you have any openings for someone at his level?'* Always tell them the reason why they should be listening to you – you have ten seconds to make a good impression.

Marketing calls are underrated. If someone contacts me saying they're from a Rec-To-Rec agency, am I going to listen to them? Probably. A lot depends on the presentation of the call. If they say, *'I've got a really great consultant here, he's relocating to Bristol after being in London for ten years, his speciality is construction, would you be interested in hearing more about him?'* of course I will be. And then if they say, *'Before I go into a little more detail, can you tell me a little bit about your company? How big is it? What do you do?'* I will probably comply, even though I realise perfectly well that they're scoping me out. They've offered me something I might want in return, so I'm happy to answer their questions. If you plan these questions ahead of the marketing call, then they'll come into the conversation more naturally. Good habits develop with experience, but so do bad ones. If someone asks, me *'Is this a good time to talk?'* it's inviting a negative response – don't present that opportunity.

Lead Call – this is similar to a Marketing Call, except you'll be acting on some specific information. You might have heard from a candidate that the company is hiring, or you might have seen on their website that they have a vacancy. The preparation for the call is the same, but the introduction might be different – more targeted at their need: *'Hi, it's James from Kingston Barnes here. We are expert construction recruiters. I noticed online you have a vacancy for a quantity surveyor. I just wanted to find out a bit more about what you're looking for, as I think I have someone who would be of interest.'*

Reference Call – this is the most enjoyable call to make – it's how we start off all of our resourcers and researchers. By taking a thorough reference, with the right introduction, you're demonstrating your diligence and professionalism to a client even when, or especially when, they haven't used your services before. *'We take our time to understand our candidates and the proof is I'm contacting you now to take a reference about xxxx.'* After you've spent five minutes building up a rapport, it's the perfect time to turn it into a sales opportunity. Ask, *'What was it that made you hire them in the first place? How did you recruit them? Would you hire them again? How do you recruit more widely? Would you consider using us for future vacancies?'* It's a nice, warm call to make – unless the candidate has absconded with the company pension fund – but it's all about the delivery again. You have to sound confident, interested and positive. I'll go into more detail about taking references in the next chapter.

So these are the four most common types of sales call. You should be aiming to make them in roughly the following proportions:

Account Management Calls – 50 per cent
Marketing Calls – 25 per cent
Lead Calls – 15 per cent
Reference Calls – 10 per cent

I can't emphasise too strongly that the key to all of them is preparation. Thinking about what you are going to say and what you want from the call is key (think MSC). Know your USPs by heart and always have a good introduction ready. Ask lots of good questions and come away with at least five bits of information you didn't have. Offer a solution to a client's problem, agree an action or commitment and actually close it. That's what a lot of people don't do. And make sure you've got a follow-up – a reason to call back.

Some people treat sales calls like something they've got to get done (through gritted teeth). They forget that there are many genuine reasons for their call and that if they've planned it well enough, the client will be glad they've made the effort. If you have a great candidate to market then it's likely the client will be happy to listen to what you have to say. And the candidate will be glad you made the effort if you end up securing them their dream job.

Remember, you are always aiming to establish a mutually beneficial relationship. The benefit doesn't have to be immediate. If they're not going to have any vacancies for three months, then you can still follow up: '*OK, when shall I call you back?*' Put a date in the diary for three months' time.

Sales doesn't need to be hard – and you don't need to go overboard in marketing a candidate – but you do need to be able to sell your company. If you can't write down and promote five USPs about the company you work for, then what are you doing there? And why would a client ever want to use you?

Top Questions to Ask a Client
What I'm going to focus on here are some really top questions to help you get the most from any sales call or client visit. These are

the questions which, over the years, I've found have helped me more than any others.

The key to any sales call is getting the information to identify a need before you present a solution. For sales, asking the right questions in the right way is key.

When you start a sales call you should use open questions as much as possible, to get a conversation going and to break any barriers or resistance you are likely to encounter. So when I'm thinking of the top questions to ask a client, these are the ones that are really going to add some value to the conversation. They will either open doors or get the result that you want – the outcomes that the Limitless Recruiter is always looking for.

1. 'Can you tell me about what you are working on at present? How is your business performing? Tell me more about what you do...'

You want to open up by engaging the individual and showing an interest in them beyond what fees they might generate. Think of it in terms of a first-date analogy – in most instances you're not going to create much of a rapport by suggesting you get married as soon as you sit down in a restaurant. It happens occasionally, but 99 per cent of the time you're going to fail. As my female Director of Construction always says, you want a bit of foreplay before you get to third base! That's exactly right. You want to get the client talking and at their ease, get the barriers down and make them more receptive to your advances.

These are open questions and can then lead you to ask more targeted questions, depending on the information you receive.

Remember, the Limitless Recruiter is always listening and reacting, never just reeling off a list of questions which, while they may potentially give you the information you need, will fail if they are not deployed with care. To return to the dating analogy, if you were sat down at dinner with someone and they read dutifully through a list of questions about your childhood, your favourite colour, your favourite sports and what you do for a living, you'd quickly be so bored that you'd be trying to catch the eye of the waiter to pay the bill and get out of there. Why should a client feel any differently?

Be prepared, then, to react if the client takes the conversation somewhere unexpected. It may be that you've called them in the middle of a recruitment crisis which they've been charged with solving immediately. If they tell you that they're desperate for five temporary staff and you plough on asking them about their turnover for the past five years, then they're going to become impatient. It's an extreme example, but you get the idea.

2. 'What are your recruitment plans over the next 12 months?'
Now you need to focus more on the specifics of why you're calling them. You're still gathering information, but you should be mentally matching your responses to the answers that they give you.

3. 'What is your biggest challenge when recruiting?'
These questions are getting the client to engage with you and probably confide often-repeated gripes which he or she shares with colleagues about the difficulties of getting the right staff.

4. 'What is the impact to your business if you don't fill this role?'

Note that all these questions involve a degree of empathy – they are showing that you not only want to understand the problems they encounter when recruiting, but also imply that you've come across similar situations many times already – you are experienced and can therefore bring your knowledge and expertise to bear on their requirements. Here, you're prompting the client to think about a negative situation for which you can provide the solution. You're not telling the client how you can help them, yet; you're getting them to think imaginatively about the problem you can solve for them. There's a big difference. It's much easier to switch off from someone telling us what a great service they can provide when we don't feel the need for that service in the first place.

5. 'What would a great service of recruitment look like to you?'

This is a great question that, if asked correctly at the right time, should yield lots of useful information for you to build on and help you set expectations for the client. You're literally asking the client to tell you what they want from you.

6. 'How do you normally recruit?'

Again, the key is finding out the information – I hope this is getting through. The Limitless Recruiter values knowledge much more than the average consultant, realising that this knowledge brings them power in the recruitment process. You need to discover the needs and wants before you present a solution. The worst salespeople just talk, they never listen. But rather than prompting the client, you are involving them.

7. 'Who is responsible for recruitment in your business?'
It might be just the person you're talking to, but it could also be someone else – the head of HR or their immediate boss, for instance. Is it the same person, or people, for temporary and permanent recruitment?

8. 'What is the ideal type of person who, if they came on the market, you would want to hear about?'
This is my all-time favourite question. You're basically asking your client to describe a candidate who, if you can find them, they will take a further interest in. This gives you the perfect 'in' to a follow-up call – *'Guess who I've got for you?'*

9. 'What can I do to get an opportunity to work with you?'
This is another favourite because, again, you're putting the onus on the client to provide you with the killer information you need. But you're doing it in such a way as to encourage them to be expansive and open up to you. It's an opportunity for them to express their frustrations with the way they usually recruit and let you know what you would have to do to improve on this.

10. 'When are you available to meet me or my candidate?'
You're not asking them, *'Can I?'* or *'Can't you?'* You're asking them, *'When?'*, *'When in your diary will you make the time?'* It's a leading or assumptive question that most people find irresistible – again, if asked at the right time. Don't barge straight in with this.

11. 'How would you like us to work together?'

This is a clever question, too, because it's a non-threatening, open question that is nevertheless leading and assumptive – you have made the jump on behalf of the client from *'Do you want to work with me?'* to *'You do, but how?'* Learn these questions off by heart and always have them in your locker. You will not regret it.

With all these questions, remember that there are a million things you can get from a sales call. If you approach it with that attitude, you will never be disappointed. The experience automatically becomes more interesting, and your enthusiasm will rub off on the client. I guarantee this – it's the growth mindset again. You might get a placement, a vacancy, or an interview – those are your ultimate goals, of course – but you may also just obtain some valuable information about the company, or the client's workload, or new points of contact. This information can be built on in subsequent calls. There's no need to rush. Alternatively, you might obtain new information about the sector, a referral or a recommendation. There's a long list of positives than can and should arise from any good sales call.

THE CLIENT VISIT

The client visit is arguably the most important part of any business development plan.

All the most successful consultants I've met have good relationships with their clients, and not just over the phone. It's the same as in real life – long-term online relationships don't work as well as face-to-face!

A client visit is your opportunity to find out all the information you need about them and tell them about you. It's your opportunity to impress them and you get to see what their company is like. This is information you can use to inspire your candidates.

The best consultants meet their candidates and clients regularly – the worst don't make it a priority. I've met every single client I've recruited for. Every client we've got a retainer with, or exclusive vacancies, or Preferred Supplier List arrangements with – guess what? I make sure I see them on a regular basis. I go to events with them. I'm part of their culture. We are seen as their partner, not simply as part of their supply chain.

To change your status, from being one of many who pesters them, to '*I'm going to be your first port of call*' – it all starts with getting yourself in front of them.

But first you need to have done your market research. As far as you can, you need to check out their financial viability. Who do they work with? What's their supply chain? When's the last time they advertised a vacancy? What do ex-employees say about the company on sites like Glassdoor? Essentially, is it worth making the journey? Some companies might take you a couple of hours to get to. Half a day spent at a company no one wants to work for is time that you shouldn't be able to afford – not if you want to be a Limitless Recruiter. This is why Market Research is so important.

Preparation
I hate to bang on about it, but preparation is key. One common mistake rookie consultants often make is not to plan their visit. They think

just by turning up and having a chat they're going to get business. It rarely works that way. Treat it the same as a sales call. Plan your questions and your MSC – your objectives for the visit. Also find out what you can about the client you're going to see – don't stalk them, but check out their LinkedIn or social media activity, and if they've written blog posts then have a quick read through. Google them – they may be in the local press for winning an award or delivering an important project. It might mean you can establish mutual interests earlier. Once you've done your preparation, check where you're going and how you're going to get there, and leave yourself enough journey time to arrive unflustered.

Introduction

The basics of a visit are the same, regardless of the sector that you are working in. An introduction to what you do – you should use this as the opportunity for a gentle sell: *'I'm here to get a better understanding of your business and how you recruit, so we can help you find the best talent in the market – which will save you a lot of time and hassle in the long run.'*

Questioning

Then fact-find with your planned questions. The worst thing you can do for any company is to start selling without first identifying their need. So, *'Tell me about your company? What are your USPs? What makes you different to the competition?'* Then talk about the individual – *'Tell me about your journey with X? When did you join? What do you like about them? What keeps you here?'* Next, recruitment – *'How do you currently recruit? What is the process? Who is involved? Have you hired much in the past 12 months? Which methods? Have you used a recruiter before? Tell me about the experience? What terms do you normally work to with them?'* Obviously, don't fire these questions at them one after the other! Give them a chance to respond. What they say may lead you in another direction, but always gently steer the conversation back to the purpose in hand. If you're just starting out, don't worry – this will become natural with practice.

You should have pages of questions on every aspect of their business, and about how and who they like to recruit. The whole purpose of the visit is to find out all the information you need in order for *you* to recruit for them.

Managing Expectations

The Limitless Recruiter will see this as just as much a question of what you shouldn't do as what you should. It's often wiser to under-promise and over-deliver – especially in the formative stages of a business relationship.

Every client will always remember the honest recruiter. But they will also remember the one that promised them the earth and then, unsurprisingly, didn't deliver. If you let a new client down – a person who has, in their mind, taken a gamble on you – then they are likely to get angry, and an emotional person will probably complain to ten times more people than someone who doesn't feel they've been deceived.

If you're the recruiter who promises the world and sometimes delivers and sometimes doesn't, then you'll get some clients who love you and some who hate you – you don't want that.

If you're consistent and honest, you will slowly build solid business relationships with your clients and candidates, which will grow stronger over time.

Trust, foundation, integrity and honesty. Tell them what you are going to do, and when, and then stick to it. If things don't go brilliantly in one particular instance, you'll be able to say honestly, *'Well, I did tell you this might happen.'* The client will respect you more for that and continue to trust your judgement.

Identify Need

While you are asking questions you need to be listening, too. Be prepared to change your line of questioning if the client flags up a need, or a frustration, and always be prepared to engage those needs with solutions. This is where good preparation pays dividends. If you know, for instance, that a particular role in that company is hard to recruit for, have the CVs of suitable candidates to hand in case the client raises this as an issue. If the client flags up that he's very busy and has little time to get involved in the recruitment process, be prepared to offer him a tailored solution – perhaps where you have exclusivity and are paid a retainer to take the process largely out of his hands.

Promote Your Agency

You then promote the company you work for. Explain your office set-up and a little about the history of the company, if it's the client's first experience of your agency. Tell them the region you cover and other details like the quality of service you provide, your costs and the fact that you'll be their main point of contact. What are your USPs – the features, advantages and benefits of using you? The client will find it much harder to ignore your calls or fob you off once they've met you in person. It's harder to hang up on someone when you've met them.

Gain Commitment

Don't be shy to ask for a commitment to yourself from the client. You will be doing them a favour, remember. People make a business and in finding them some great candidates you will be helping their business to deliver and grow. You will be adding real value and freeing them up to concentrate on their work. When you've found the need, what do you do? If there's a vacancy, you talk about that. Take a detailed job spec, agree a timeline and an action plan. Rather than say, *'I'll send you some CVs'* if it's going to be a hard vacancy to fill, pitch a retainer or book some interview slots for a couple of weeks' time. If it's easy, book them for a couple of days' time. If it's a temporary role, you could even agree a start time for a candidate you already have in mind. It'll motivate you to work so much harder to find the right candidates. I always ask for a retainer first. If the answer is 'no', then I ask for exclusivity on the position. If that's a 'no' then at the very least ask, *'Are you happy to work with us?'* If so, *'Great, here are our terms.'*

Agree Action

If you're taking a vacancy during the visit, agree a timescale for recruitment and get that commitment to use your services. Check that you can send CVs on spec for quality candidates. If there is no immediate vacancy, agree a call-back time – a weekly, monthly or quarterly check-in. Ask them to commit to giving you 24 hours with any vacancy before contacting another agency.

Visits are the most important part of any recruiter's day. Every consultant should be going out at least 2–5 times a week to meet clients. Some of our recruiters are out on site two days a week, meeting 20+ people. Relationships are built face-to-face.

Negotiating Fees

My golden rule for negotiating fees is to have the conversation at the earliest possible time. At lot of recruiters put it off for as long as possible – until the offer of an interview or, worse still, the offer of a job. This is a bad tactic. You need to do it when you are still in a position of relative power – before you've expended any time or energy on recruiting for a vacancy, you need to know on what terms you are doing so. As soon as you get to the endgame, all the power is with the client.

Get it done.

Do it face-to-face if you can – you can read your client better and it also *never feels so combative in person.*

The best way to negotiate is to **start high**. First a proviso: by this stage, you should have found out about your client's recruitment practices, including what level of fees they are usually charged and their rebate structure. If you've discovered that they've got 25 agencies on the PSL at 15 per cent, and you come in at 25 per cent, are they going to use you? They might consider you for one-off vacancy, but the aim of this negotiation isn't a one-night stand. You want an ongoing and developing business relationship.

If it's the first question they ask you about – which might well be the case if they're in HR – you still need to find out what cards they're holding before you reveal your hand. If you say, *'Our fees are 15 per cent,'* and they say, *'We normally pay 20 per cent, so that's great,'* then you've lost 5 per cent straight away. So always answer that question with *'What are you currently paying and what service do you get?'*

Don't be afraid to ask for more than they are used to, within reason. Know your worth – know how valuable your time is and believe in it. People who don't think their time is valuable, or don't think that the service they offer is exceptional – they'll do it for anything. If you do charge more, it's not a problem as long as you are prepared and confident about justifying it (which you should be able to do by now). If you don't know and they won't tell you what they are charged before hearing your terms, then pitch it at a level that you feel happy justifying anyway.

But always start high. You can compromise, if necessary, on other parts of your terms, like the rebate period for example, but if you start low you can't go up. It's almost a law of physics. Give the client your figure and then don't speak. Just wait for their response. The next person to speak is usually the one who ends up compromising. Know your worth, when to be flexible and when to say 'no' and walk away.

You can be flexible once the relationship is underway. We have a client who gives us 50 vacancies a year, on average. For this we have offered a sliding scale that discounts the fee with every ten placements because we know that when we send them a CV, the candidate will start with them. The process is quicker and slicker. Our relationship is that good. It's worth the slight drop in income to keep things running smoothly, with both parties feeling that they are getting a good deal. This is the state of play you should be aiming towards at all times.

Don't let emotions get in the way. The worst decisions ever made are when emotions are high. Know your head, know your heart, but trust your gut. If you're feeling emotional about a situation, don't let that cloud your judgement. Take your time – you don't have to agree there and then. If the client says something, or suggest terms which you consider an insult, then take a deep breath and say, *'Give me 24 hours to think about it.'* Sleep on it. Discuss it with colleagues and your manager. Think about your personal life: in any major relationship there are conflicts and you or your partner say things you wish you hadn't. It's the same in recruitment. Quite often when you are negotiating fees it will get like this towards the end. Let the emotions run low. Remove yourself.

Empathise first – *'I completely hear what you're saying. Let me talk to my manager…and come back to you.'* Give it 24 hours. Don't ever be afraid to say no and walk away. We will never work below 10 per cent – ever. Even if we are potentially losing lots of vacancies, we know that the level of service we offer is worth more than that. By the same token, if you're struggling to win any clients because your company is charging too much, then it's time to discuss a new approach and revisit your fees.

If you're working in the kind of cut-throat market where everyone is working at the same low level, it can be hard to elevate yourself above the rest. But you should always be able to put a value on what you do – by service, by results, by recommendations.

The number of times we get a call from a client who says, *'We were in touch six months ago. You know that other agency we decided to go with instead of you, because their terms were a bit lower? It didn't really work out. Can you come and help us?'*

'Yes, that's great but our fees are the same as they were. Are you happy with that?'

A Limitless Recruiter will be able to negotiate their own fees. *'How valuable is great recruitment to your business?'* Highlight the USPs of your service.

VACANCY REGISTRATION

There are essentially two types of vacancy registration – temporary and permanent. In either case, the aim must be to get every single bit of information you are going to need to identify the best candidate, sell the opportunity and then get the candidate the job.

Many recruiters make a sales call or go on a visit and return to the office jubilant that they've got a vacancy to fill from the client. That's how it should be, but some consultants get so excited that they forget to ask all the really important details, like finding out how far along the recruitment process is, agreeing terms and conditions, or getting the full job specification.

Take Details

Most companies will have a template listing key questions you should ask while registering a vacancy. It should cover the basics:

- Position – responsibilities, location, hours, reporting structure
- Person – qualifications, experience, skills required
- Package – salary, company car, overtime, training offered, prospects
- Benefits – holiday, pension, private medical, share scheme and any other perks.

But if you really want the get to the bones of a vacancy you need to dig deeper. It's not enough to ask about the day-to-day duties and get the basics. To help you fill a role, match better and sell the opportunity to potential candidates, you need more detail to qualify a vacancy and be able to deliver. The kind of information that will really assist a savvy recruiter includes:

- What are the three most important duties, in priority order?
- What specific objectives will this person be expected to achieve?
- How will these be measured?
- Who had this position last?
- Why did they leave?
- How long had they been with the company?
- What was their background?
- Where are they now?
- Describe the best person you've had doing this role?

- How ambitious should the ideal person be? When do you envisage promotion?
- What are the next steps for this person?
- What are the long-term opportunities in, for example, three or five years?
- Which companies or industries do you like people to come from, and why?
- Are there any other industries you would consider?
- Which companies do you not like people to come from, and why?
- Are there any individuals (target candidates) whom you would like to be included in this recruitment process? If so, why?

As I've said before, one question I love asking is, *'Tell me what the perfect candidate would look like to you?'* or, *'Is there someone in your business you'd like them to be a mirror image of? Tell me about that person....'*

When it comes to skills, we really want to know what is desired vs. essential; what the candidate must have to do the job and cannot do the job without. A wish list is always a good way to approach this – *'What, ideally, would you like, but not necessarily need?'*

Other things that will help include getting a background on the previous/current job holder when they started the job. If the job is too specific, then to increase your chances of success you need to know if there are any skills that are substitutable or transferable? Or which parts of this role could be trained?

You can proactively prevent a placement falling apart over

negotiations by asking a simple question, *'How much flexibility is there over the salary?'* If you find the perfect candidate, but they're on £xxx more than the stated salary, will the client be willing to better it?

A Limitless Recruiter will only work on a vacancy they know they can fill, but which they also know a client will hire for if they send the right candidate. When taking a vacancy, we are as much finding out about the client as we are about the position. So in addition to the job specification, we need to be looking at the company's attractiveness to help us promote the role. You need to ask about the following:

- Company Background / Turnover / Profit for the past three years
- Number of employees
- Key customers
- How quickly have you (the client) and other staff been promoted?
- Growth plans and areas of future development?
- Why would a happily-employed person want to work in this role?
- How would you describe your company's image?
- Any planned new products / services / innovations?
- Who are the main competitors?
- What are you doing better than them?
- Why did you join the company personally? (Where did you work previously?)

Lastly, and most importantly, there is the recruitment process. Knowing exactly where your client is in the process will instantly put a tick or cross in the 'should I work on this vacancy?' box. I will not let any recruiter at my agency work on a role if they do not know the answer to the following three questions:

- Why has the vacancy arisen?
- How long has the vacancy been open and what steps have been taken to fill it so far?
- Have you looked internally? Has the budget been signed off?

Then, to make sure no time is wasted (time management is a key strand to the DNA of a Limitless Recruiter), we need to question the client's process of recruitment. We need to know where they are in the process, in order to assess how much time (if any) we should be spending on a role, and so we are in a position to grade the vacancy. If there is only one other agency recruiting for it, but the vacancy has been open for six months, you need to find out why it hasn't been filled. If the vacancy only arose the previous week, but they have 20 other agencies looking for them, is it going to be worth your time? How urgent is it? If you find them someone tomorrow, how soon could they start them? What's the recruitment procedure and when can they interview? These are all vital questions that will not only help you fill the vacancy more efficiently, but also show the client that you are professional and you know what you're doing. So when taking a vacancy, make sure you know the following:

- What is the usual interview procedure – how many interviews are there? Does the client use any other processes of assessment, like psychometric testing or a medical?
- How long after the first interview will the second meeting take place?
- Who else will be involved in the interviews?
- What is their background/personality?
- Who is the ultimate decision-maker?
- When are they available for the first interviews – earliest and latest times?
- Will the interview be in person, online or over the phone?
- What other recruiting sources are they currently using (in-house, adverts, other recruiters)?
- How many people have they interviewed so far (including internally)?
- How many CVs have they received? What have they liked and disliked about the people they've interviewed and the CVs they've seen?
- Can they describe the best candidate/CV they've seen?
- Has an offer been rejected for this role? If so, why?

As with any other recruitment process, always summarise the details back to the client to check you've got everything right and then agree a course of action, with specific dates and measurables. Congrats – you've qualified a vacancy to a Limitless Recruiter standard.

THE ART OF RECRUITMENT

Grading Vacancies

In a busy market with lots of vacancies it's easy to get bogged down and lost in the abyss. But looking at the wider picture is vital if you want to be a Limitless Recruiter. If you're going to spend some of your valuable time on a vacancy, it needs to be worth it – you need to know you've got the best chance of making a success of it.

Many recruiters struggle to prioritise which vacancies to work on. Some lean towards clients they like, others to whichever positions are the most interesting, different or popular – or simply the ones they feel most comfortable with. Many recruiters just work on the most recent vacancy they have picked up, perhaps from a new client. The problem with this approach is that it's not necessarily the most efficient, and certainly not a method that will get you performing at your peak.

The most efficient way of managing your vacancies is to grade them. Firstly, take a step back and ask yourself these key questions about your vacancy list:

- Have I got enough information?
- Do I want to be working on it?
- Should I be working on it?

That will get you thinking before you leap. But to take it one step further, we need a measurable method – to help you put a number on and rank all your jobs on a list, so that you can focus your attention where it should be. Realistically a consultant can only work on so many jobs at any one time, no matter how good they are. So by placing all your jobs in order of merit, you should end up only working on the right vacancies with the highest chance of placing. Whenever we take a vacancy, I get the consultant to grade it 1–10 (10 for best, 1 for worst), on seven different aspects:

1) *Client* – is the client attractive to work for? How do they rank in their particular sector?

2) *Role* – will it appeal to a range of candidates? Is it a desirable role? Where would you rank it among your current vacancies?

3) *Terms* – are the terms agreed? 10 per cent? 20 per cent? How do they rank alongside other client terms?

4) *Exclusivity* – how many other agencies are you up against? If you're the only agency working on it, that's a '10'. If you're up against ten other agencies and the client has their own internal team working on it, then grade it as a '1'.

5) *Fillability!* – Will it be like trying to find a brain surgeon in Skegness, or is it a vacancy for which you could supply three good candidates after a couple of hours' work? Give the brain surgery a '1'.

6) *Timescale/urgency* – How urgent is it that the client fills the vacancy? Will you get their full attention and cooperation because they needed it filled yesterday? Or are they going through the motions? '10' for yesterday, '1' for the motions.

7) *Commitment* – is the client going to do what they say they're going to do? When we send people over, will they agree to see them? Do they usually offer straight after they've seen a good candidate? Or do they take weeks to come back to you?

Only work on the Grade A vacancies – those with a total score of 49 or above. If you think there's going to be a problem then set expectations with the client. Agree a deadline you'll both work to.

You'll know instinctively, after a while, whether a vacancy is a good one or not. Every week, I get my consultants to go through their vacancies and pick two or three Grade A roles to concentrate on. It focuses their minds and it also means they regularly have a new challenge to rise to. These are also the roles that will guarantee you your interviews for the week and lead to a higher interview-to-placement ratio.

Remember, things change all the time, so grade and prioritise but also re-evaluate your vacancies periodically. If you've got a 'live' vacancy, you should be in touch with the client once or twice a week. This is to touch base on the progress you've made and also to keep tabs that the client hasn't given out the vacancy to five other agencies. After a few weeks, a client might increase the salary they're willing to pay. Or they might be persuadable to getting temporary cover for the role, to tide them over a particularly busy period. Roles that a client has been actively trying to fill for six months might be a great opportunity to pitch a retainer, as it's likely everyone involved in the process is a bit stale and a renewed, invigorated approach might increase the chances of the client finding someone suitable.

The key to registering a vacancy, then, is all about making sure you take enough details to sell to a candidate, but also about you being aware of where it fits into your wider workload and objectives. You need to obtain every single bit of information required to ensure that you have the highest chance of success in filling the role. But nothing is more guaranteed of a finder's fee than a retainer...

RETAINERS

When you mention the word 'retainer' – or talk about 'retained recruitment' or a 'retained assignment' – most recruiters instantly visualise an executive search consultancy producing inch-thick reports to recruit board-level positions on six- or seven-figure salaries, and they'd be right. Talent acquisition for senior positions within large corporations usually does involve a company engaging with an executive search firm. But retained recruitment isn't just limited to corporate head-hunters, or only used for senior appointments.

As I write this book, the number of job vacancies in the UK right now has topped one million. In a candidate-led market, where you are inundated with job vacancies, it's very easy for a recruiter to be busy. But a contingent recruiter with a list of live vacancies as long as their arm is likely to have a very poor fill ratio of placements to vacancies. What if there was a way to reduce the amount of time wasted on vacancies, increase exclusive vacancies, improve relationships with clients and throw in the benefits of guaranteed revenue and higher fees?

Say hello to retained recruitment.

What is a Retained Assignment? How is it different to Contingent Recruitment?

A retained assignment is basically what it says on the tin. A recruiter is 'retained' to conduct a specific piece of recruitment, with a financial commitment from a client.

In retained recruitment, the recruiter is paid an upfront or scheduled fee and works on an exclusive basis, meaning that only they should be looking for a candidate – and dedicating all their time and resources to filling the position.

By contrast, contingency recruitment works on what would be best described as a 'no win, no fee' basis. If they find and place a candidate, they get paid. If they don't, they won't. A typical permanent contingent recruiter will work on anywhere between five and forty positions for a variety of clients, often against multiple recruiters (internal and external), to find the right talent. 'Contingent', by definition, means subject to chance which, if you think about it, can be quite a daunting feeling for a budding recruiter – your success being purely down to luck. But this should never be the case, especially for a Limitless Recruiter! Always having the right weapons in your armoury, and knowing when to use them, is key to mastering the art of recruitment. Using retainers as an additional revenue stream is something every recruiter should consider.

There is nothing wrong with contingency recruitment – at Kingston Barnes it's our bread and butter. But to make sure we have a constant pipeline of permanent revenue, we offer a mix of both approaches. This is sensible. Retained recruitment can also elevate your partnerships within client organisations. This is because in contingent recruitment, it is usually the operational staff – not those at board level – who deal with these vacancies. Retained assignments tend to bring you into contact with directors and business leaders. Your ultimate goal as a recruiter should be to form strategic partnerships with these people and develop trusted advisor status with them. Retained recruitment will help you do this, as long as you produce the goods!

Typically, the retained assignment process is not actually very different to contingent recruitment, other than the amount of time spent, and how the activity is presented and invoiced. If you work for an executive search firm you'll disagree, of course. Often, mountains of research are undertaken, with reports detailing competitor analysis, market trends, salary surveys and all the activity completed throughout the assignment. But the really interesting thing is, if you put yourself in the client's shoes, what do you really want? It's the juicy stuff: the output of finding the right candidate and seeing enough suitable people who have been identified and vetted, and will accept a position if and when you offer it – so the measurables are virtually identical.

How Are the Payments Structured?

A retained recruitment assignment doesn't come cheap. The client can expect to pay up to 50 per cent of the projected first annual salary of the successful candidate. While this may sound expensive, contingency recruitment fees are usually 10–30 per cent. So if the role is difficult to recruit for, retained recruitment may actually prove more cost-effective if it produces exactly the right candidate first time. And what would the cost be to the client if no-one was in post at all?

So it can be surprisingly cost-effective. At Kingston Barnes, for instance, our success rate for retained assignments is close to 100 per cent, compared to the industry average for contingency placements, which is around 38 per cent.

A retained assignment fee is structured differently to a contingency search, to enable the recruitment consultant to dedicate more resources, time and effort in filling the position. The fee is usually split into thirds, which are paid at the following stages:

Stage 1 – the first payment is due at the beginning, when the employer and recruitment consultant agree to work the vacancy on a retained assignment basis. This works as a guarantee and enables the consultant to concentrate their time and effort on this prioritised position.

Stage 2 – the second third is due when the employer has a shortlist of candidates whom they would like to interview for the position.

Stage 3 – the third and final payment is due upon completion of the assignment, when the selected candidate has commenced employment.

Benefits to the Client

For the client, the benefits are clear. A retained search usually goes further and deeper than a typical contingency search, with a much higher chance of success. Industry research suggests consultants spend five to ten times the amount of time on a retained vacancy.

Winning and Delivering a Retainer

The key to winning and delivering a retainer is to know when and how to use it. The first trick for any recruiter wanting to bag their first retainer is to identify a suitable vacancy. This is one where you can pitch to the client for the opportunity to deliver a retained assignment as the right solution to their need. The best place to start looking for a retainer is actually within your existing portfolio of clients. Retained recruitment works best when a company has important positions, or ones that are difficult to fill. Given the strategic importance of these positions, there is often a degree of urgency and confidentiality accompanying this type of search. So taking our slightly tweaked grading system for prioritising vacancies, go through your current list with a retainer hat on and rank each vacancy 1–10 for each of the following criteria, then total the results:

1. Length of time the client has been looking *(1: today; 10: six months)*
2. 'Fillability' – how easy is the role to fill, niche skillset *(1: easy to fill; 10: only a handful of people on the planet)*
3. New role for the client or new market they are entering *(1: existing role in existing business; 10: new position in a whole new market)*
4. Urgency of the vacancy *(1: whenever; 10: yesterday)*
5. Negative perception of client *(1: household name; 10: worst name in the market)*
6. Confidential hire *(1: tell the world; 10: not a word to anyone)*
Location *(1: major city centre, easy access and appealing location; 10: remote desert island)*

7.Senior Position *(1: basic, low-level role; 10: most senior position in the company)*.

So, with a potential score of 70, what vacancies do you have that are over 60? These are your starting-point.

The Pitch and Proposal

After identifying a client's potential need for a retainer, book a face-to-face visit. Set an agenda and send it to the client prior to the meeting, so that you're in control of the process. *Preparation is key.* Research as much information as possible about the business – contacts, office knowledge and any problems you can uncover with their history of recruitment or staff retention. The visit is no different to any other in terms of its structure, but with your retainer hat on, you need to ensure your questioning and qualification is planned with this in mind. Find out everything you can about the client – their situation and the business. Ask problem-solving questions about issues with staffing – recruitment and retention.

Use Active listening. 80 per cent of your visit should be listening and consulting – not selling. Remember, if you're going to ask for someone to pay upfront for a new service, making the right first impression and building a rapport is vital. You need them to feel that they know you, like you and, most importantly, trust you to deliver. *Present the retained solution.* Solve the identified problems. Explain what your agency does and how you do it, highlighting case studies, success rates and any USPs. Maybe how you have helped clients in a similar situation. Then, based on what you have talked about, how does the service compare to contingency? You should have shown that it is a more efficient and productive way to work with your retained solution. The gap between these services can then be used to explain the gap between the fees for each option. How does that sound?

Closing and Delivering

The hardest part is usually getting a 'yes'. You've listened, questioned, pitched and now you're about to receive the verdict on your performance. So, summarise key problems identified – and aim to get 2–3 'yeses'. *'What you are saying, then, is that these are your problems, and if you had a solution this would be of benefit? That it's really important to have this role filled soon, otherwise your division won't be able to deliver on its targets?'* When it comes to asking for the up-front fee, be confident. Your fee is based on the level of service – the client is simply paying more for a better level of service. You will likely hear objections and the client may want to negotiate. Beware that negotiating the fee suggests that you don't think the service you're offering is worth it, and that is what the client will be thinking the whole time. Will you be able to deliver? If the answer is no, then don't pitch it. Just go for exclusivity and a traditional contingency approach. If it's a firm 'yes', then you should be on your way to your first retained assignment.

When Not to Sell a Retainer

It's important to know when *not* to sell a retainer, too!

If the vacancy is easy to fill – then retained recruitment might be a little like using a sledgehammer to crack a nut. The client may also not trust your judgement if you suggest an exclusive, high fee arrangement to fill such a position.

If the vacancy is impossible to fill – no vacancy should be impossible to recruit for, but if the client is really inflexible about the parameters of the role, won't commit to the description, or is simply unpleasant to deal with, you might be better off working on contingency terms.

If you're inexperienced – it's important to have some experience of contingency recruitment and be confident you can actually deliver! You need to be able to demonstrate that you know the recruitment process because this is what you'll be selling against – so an understanding of why it is or isn't working for a particular vacancy, and why a retainer is the right solution, is essential.

THE LIMITLESS RECRUITER WILL...
- **Know everything about the sector they are recruiting in and the roles they are recruiting for**
- **Ensure they have two or three referenced candidates to hand for every marketing or spec call**
- **Make sure they make a good spread of the four types of sales call – Account Management, Marketing, Lead and Reference – each and every week**
- **Regularly grade and prioritise their vacancies**
- **Ask every client they visit if they will work with them exclusively**

- Always be prepared to engage a client's needs with solutions
- Know that the key to any sales call is thorough preparation
- Be going out at least 2–5 times a week to meet clients
- Always have an agenda for a sales call or a client visit – the 'MSC'
- Rehearse a ten-second introduction for any call until it is perfect
- Know when, and when not, to pitch retained recruitment
- Use retained recruitment to elevate their partnerships within client organisations.

Chapter Six:
The Interview and Beyond

'Choose a job you love, and you will never have to work a day in your life.' – Confucius

- Presenting CVs to the Client
- Candidate Interview Preparation
- Debriefing Clients
- Offer Presentation and Negotiation
- Resignation Briefing

The key to achieving interviews is firstly and obviously to have the right candidates, but you must also be able to present them to your client in such a way that they will and must need to see them. It's a bit of an art – a skill you pick up with experience. In other words, as I've said before, your knowledge of your industry, the sector you are working in, the client and your candidate is all-important.

So, you're at the point where you have a live vacancy and you have a candidate you want your client to meet. This is how you present a candidate's CV – preferably on the phone or face-to-face – to ensure you'll get an interview.

PRESENTING CVS TO THE CLIENT

After you have interviewed your candidate, you should know enough about them and the types of roles they are suitable for. You should be familiar with their track record, motivators and career ambitions, as well as their strengths and weaknesses. For a refresher, read the section on Candidate Registration.

The first stage is to prepare a profile of the candidate, at least one hundred words. This applies whether you are working in contingent recruitment, marketing a candidate speculatively, or working on a retainer. Like a profile for a dating website, you want the profile to contain all the good stuff and present your candidate in the best light. You want it to prompt your client to agree to your call to action, which is basically to get the candidate in front of them.

Your purpose will dictate the kind of introduction used. If you're speccing a candidate, you might begin with, *'I've got a really good candidate, I think he might be of interest to you'*. If you've already registered a vacancy then, *'Thank you for the role, I've found someone suitable, this is her'*. If you are delivering a retainer the key is to highlight the strengths and suitability of all the candidates you are proposing. This is the whole point of preparing a CV for a client. Note – if you're presenting the CV 'on spec' you might not want to divulge the candidate's name yet, just in case he is known by the client, or just to safeguard your interests.

The bulk of the profile will be the same in each scenario. I always follow the same structure. I've written an example below and then outlined, in layman's terms, how to write a great profile.

THE ART OF RECRUITMENT

Presenting a CV

Introduction – *length depends on whether contingency, speculative or retainer*

Identify Candidate by Job Title or Company – *level of detail divulged depends on the purpose of the call*

Benefit – *how the candidate will fit into and improve the client's team*

Achievements – *brief overview of the candidate's **relevant** accomplishments to date*

Reasons for Changing – ***positive** reasons why a candidate is keen to leave current job and apply to your client*

Education – *brief details highlighting any exceptional achievements*

Create Excitement – *reasons why the client should see this candidate **now** – not next week*

Set Interview Appointment – *or appointments, especially if working on a retainer.*

Sample Profile

If a recruiter is marketing a consultant to another recruiter then the profile might read, or sound, something like this:

'Joe B is someone I feel would be perfect for your business and add real value. He is a Bristol-based Principal Consultant eager to be considered for a position with you. Joe has been in recruitment for ten years with the same employer. He has worked his way up from Trainee to Principal Consultant for John Smith Consulting, recruiting within the construction sector and covering the whole of the UK for roles from trainee quantity surveyor to £250k board director appointments.

Joe has built up a division from scratch to a client base of over 50 key accounts including top 100 FTSE companies, regional contractors, and national developers. He has consistently delivered £250k of permanent revenue, placing between 40 and 50 candidates per year. He is regarded as one of the best in his company, having won consultant of the year in 2017 and 2018, and is the second-highest biller in a company of fifty.

Joe feels he has hit a ceiling and there is no room for opportunity with his current employer to progress to the next level. He is keen to find a role that can offer more of the market he is currently working in and a role that will enable him to develop a team and a division, and take his career towards a path of management and directorship in the future.

Joe is on £35k basic with a £5k car allowance. This year he earned £65k in total. He is keen to progress forward so ideally wants a base around £40–45k with further performance-based bonuses available. He is working with us exclusively and can see you next Monday to Friday between 5 pm and 6 pm.

There is interest in Joe from other companies, so I would urge you to meet him as soon as possible, as a candidate of his calibre will not be on the market for long.'

How to Write a Great Profile

You must make the client aware of every single thing they need to know about the candidate at this stage. Here is a checklist:

• Candidate's name, or the job title if you want to keep it confidential

- Location
- Application method (e.g. via your website, via your database, or head-hunted specifically for the role, etc.)
- Years of experience
- The position the candidate is in and an overview of the role
- Overview of key employers
- A brief summary of the candidate's career, highlighting notable achievements and anything else relevant to your client's vacancy
- Key measurables and why they would be applicable to the vacancy
- Why the candidate is looking
- Current remuneration and motivators
- Interview availability and current interview status.

Leave anything negative until the end. It's just common sense. If someone calls me and starts off with, *'Hi James, you're probably not going to want to talk to me, but...'*, I'll immediately be on the back foot and expecting the worst. Similarly, if you introduce the candidate by saying, *'Look, he's had three jobs in the past three years, but...'* then a client will immediately be suspicious of the candidate's worth and you'll have to talk them back up, which is always much harder. As in life, it's generally best to cover the good stuff first.

Not everyone is perfect. Not everyone can be the dream candidate. Typically, you'll meet a candidate who your gut instinct and research tell you will be a good fit at the company you're marketing to, but frankly, their CV looks all over the place. You have to persuade the client not to take their CV at face value. This is why I can't emphasise enough – *'ring, don't ping'*.

Here's an example. I was recently sent the CV of a graduate for a trainee consultant role. All it was consisted of was a list of the schools and colleges he'd been to, and his exam grades. No aspect of it was factually wrong but what did it tell me about the person? Nothing.

'The Limitless Recruiter will always go the extra mile in digging down to find out what the candidate's special achievements are – why they stand out from similarly experienced applicants. And you need to make sure you can convey these achievements in a conversation or email to your client.' – James Kingston

---

So, I said to the recruiter, *'Tell me why we should employ this guy? What's he done out of school?'* You wouldn't believe his achievements. This graduate played every sport known to man. He was a county-level tennis player. He had a black belt in martial arts, and bronze, silver and gold Duke of Edinburgh's Awards. He had been constantly testing himself and pushing his boundaries outside of academia. I hadn't been made aware of any of this by the consultant.

It's the same with most candidates. Everyone does their day job and most people tick the boxes on a job spec for day-to-day duties. But it's your job, as the Limitless Recruiter, to highlight their particular, individual successes in perhaps only a minute-long conversation with your client.

Before you send the CV to a client look at it and ask yourself,

What would I think if I received this? There's no point doing the greatest sales call in the world, but then the client spots something about the candidate that doesn't add up and that you hadn't already covered. You need to be aware of any apparent shortcomings and be able to explain them to the client. You need to anticipate what the client is going to think and counteract it ahead of them.

For example, imagine the candidate has had three jobs in three years. It may transpire that in one of them the company went into administration. The second job may have offered a massive salary increase that attracted him, but the increase was there for a reason – it was a horrible job, the company was dysfunctional and that's why they were having to pay over the odds. If you find out the reasons and explain them in a positive light the client is not going to look at the candidate negatively, as they might do after only a cursory glance at their CV.

I had a project manager once who was involved in a project which notoriously lost an absurd amount of money – anyone affiliated with it was immediately tarnished. As a consultant you need to be able to deal with that. His was an entry-level role so he wasn't in any way responsible and in fact he did a good job. But without this being explained, the fact that he had worked on that project might have counted against him. Always check, always explain.

When presenting the CV this is also the time to prepare the client for any issues they may encounter when meeting the candidate. It may be that you have a great candidate who has a nervous tic, or a stutter, or gets incredibly nervous in an interview situation despite their best efforts. This doesn't mean they won't be a brilliant, high-performing employee. Most clients, if they're forewarned, will not judge a candidate on such things. If they do, then your candidate might be better off not working for them anyway.

Salary expectations are another frequent bone of contention. Make sure the client and the candidate are at least on the same page when it comes to figures, or you're wasting everyone's time. Sure, there may be an exceptional candidate that a client will move heaven and earth to accommodate, but the reality is usually a little harsher. It's all about communication, transparency and thoughtfulness.

'The Limitless Recruiter will make sure that both parties know all the facts and details necessary to secure the candidate and secure the position.' – James Kingston

---

Remember, you're not looking to alter the facts but simply to present them in the best way – to show your candidate in the best light. Ultimately, if a candidate isn't right for the job, or he doesn't fit into the company, then he's not going to get the job regardless. But the Limitless Recruiter can make a difference by ensuring that he gets a fair hearing – that the client isn't rejecting him because his CV does not present his strengths and best qualities. That is the bare minimum you should be doing for someone who has entrusted you with representing them to potential employers.

THE ART OF RECRUITMENT

Before You Present a Candidate to a Client, Here's a Checklist…
- Have you interviewed?
- Have you referenced?
- Have you got a CV?
- Have you obtained the candidate's permission to send their CV and discuss them with a client exclusively?
- Have you written a profile?
- Have you anticipated any problems the client might raise?
- What are the candidate's key strengths and achievements?
- Why should the client see them now?

Multiple Candidates

If you have two or more candidates to present in the same conversation or email, you need to shorten the profiles and differentiate them clearly (this is more applicable in situations where you've picked up a vacancy, rather than when you're speccing a candidate). Highlight their collective strengths (their suitability for the role, their shared experience), then highlight their individual achievements – what makes them different from each other – and, crucially, why are you presenting them together? What added value in impact is it going to give the client? Different personalities? Outlooks? Outline their major selling points in advance – that always works really well.

If you're presenting your candidates face-to-face, because you've arranged a meeting to discuss a vacancy, then you need to have a little bit of urgency about you. Create FOMO – a fear of missing out – in the client so that you can arrange the interviews right away. Give the client a reason why they need to see your candidates – and quickly. *'There is considerable interest in all three candidates, as you can appreciate with this level of experience – and in the market as it currently is.'* Create excitement, desire, urgency.

PREPARING CANDIDATES FOR INTERVIEW

So, you've done all the legwork, and sent the candidate's CV over, having presented them to the client. The client likes what she sees and invites them in for interview. You arrange the date and time. Now you have to prepare the candidate for the interview.

The general rule is, the more senior the position, the more prepping you need to do. But take it from me, if you had the time to prepare every candidate equally well, you would make a lot more placements.

'The Limitless Recruiter will prep the candidate so well that they've practically got the job before they walk in the door.' –
James Kingston

You need to make sure the candidate knows all about the company, what they do, how they do it, the key people, the key projects, who their clientele are. They need to know that company inside and out.

As a recruiter you cannot completely determine the outcome of the interview, so you must influence the parts of the process that you can. You can probably tip the odds in your favour by 20–30 per cent maximum if the client is seeing multiple candidates. In my agency, we have a 1:1.25 interview placement success ratio. This means that for every five interviews we arrange, on average four are offered on. It's a very good ratio and that's because we leave nothing to chance that we can possibly influence.

It's in your hands.

The only real exception to this is that if it's the first time you've sent a candidate to be interviewed with a particular client, there will be a limit to how much detail you can give them. Just do as much as you can and then thoroughly debrief the candidate afterwards. Then use this knowledge to your benefit in subsequent interviews with that client.

The worst recruiters are the ones who just arrange an interview and hope for the best. Fingers crossed, eyes closed, head in the sand. Eight times out of ten, it's not going to happen. Or pot luck – leaving it to chance.

The Limitless Recruiter is always looking at the process and thinking, *What can I do to influence it to my benefit and success?* Always.

Don't leave the prep to the last minute – the day before or even an hour before – as I've seen consultants do. The chances are the candidate won't take in any of the information at that stage and you run the risk of panicking them.

The Limitless Recruiter will have done enough research on the client to be able to get the candidate to want to go and see them in the first place. Again, there is no substitute for a client visit in this regard. The extra details you will pick up about the offices, the ambience, the other workers are priceless.

I went to see a client who was a contractor working for a multi-national. The multi-national liked all their contractors to be smart – in a shirt and tie – as they felt it reflected a professional attitude. So it was important to the client that any candidates we sent should be well turned out. But furthermore, he told me he didn't like it when the staff left their top button undone. It's the sort of detail that would emerge only in face-to-face conversation – it would have sounded petty on the phone – but I made sure that all our candidates dressed accordingly. As a consequence, we developed a great working relationship. Another client I know can't stand beards. It's tough, but there you go. I had a candidate who was very keen to work at his company and I told him, *'If you want the job, you're going to have to go the extra mile and shave your beard off.'* He did and he got the job.

Presentations

Some candidates you have to go to the next level with. I always expect interviewees to give a presentation on the sector they're going to be working in and for senior roles in many different sectors, a presentation is becoming an increasingly common part of the interview process. It may very well be worth your while to sit in while your candidate rehearses their presentation – or at least offer to do this. You may not understand all the content but your expertise, as the Limitless Recruiter, is with presentation skills and so you may be able to offer some useful guidance here. This will only strengthen the bond between you and the candidate. You should also know a lot more about the client and their company than the candidate, to be able to correct any minor misconceptions or suggest additions to the presentation which you know will be well-received during the interview.

Worse-case scenario at a senior level – even if they don't get the job, they may well end being a client.

So, the essentials.

Attire

Make sure your candidate is aware of what counts as suitable attire with the client. If they are going for a labouring job it may not be an issue – but check anyway. Personally, I prefer someone who overdresses, but you can go too far. If you dress too smartly you might make the client feel threatened! And someone dressed in a charcoal three-piece suit with a satin red tie is going to feel like a fish out of water if everyone is wearing floral print shirts and chinos. Use your judgement and knowledge of the client. Advise accordingly.

Location and Journey

This can be as basic as where the client's office is, how long it will take them to get there and any likely traffic delays. What's the best route? Will they be able to park on the premises? If not, is there ample parking nearby? Is there a bus or tube strike? All these details can be checked in an instant online, so it's pretty unforgiveable for the candidate to go unbriefed. You might reasonably expect the candidate to check these things for themselves, and they probably will, but you need to be sure that they have. If there's a bit of time before the interview, and the location is hard to get to or out of the way, suggest that they do a dummy run, so that there's one less thing for them to worry about on the day.

Oh, and always make sure that they have your number and the client's number. There might be an accident en route and you need the candidate to be able to contact the client directly to explain, in case they can't get hold of you for some reason.

'Mid-morning midweek is the optimum time to arrange an interview. On Mondays and Fridays, people are either rushing in or out of the offices, and mid-morning means you avoid the rush hours.' – James Kingston

---

Research

The worst candidates rock up, show no knowledge or interest in the company's history or performance, are totally passive and when asked if they have any questions respond, *'No, I think you've covered everything.'* Good candidates are engaged and interested enough to have done their own research, which is always the best kind. You can encourage them and check that they are going in the right direction by asking, *'What do you know about the company? Can you give me three reasons why you would like to work there?'*

The Limitless Recruiter will take this a stage further. For any substantial position, I fill the candidate in on the actual client – what they're like, how long they've been at the company, why they like working there – their likes and dislikes. If they share a love of the same football team, or holiday destination, or another hobby like cycling or the opera then great. Anything that provides the client and the candidate with common ground will help the interview process to flow more smoothly, which can only be a good thing. You're adding value to the research they ought to be doing themselves.

This applies most acutely to younger candidates who may have very little interview experience and may find the whole process nerve-wracking, thereby not showing themselves to their best advantage.

Behaviour

There are several absolute 'no-no's which any self-respecting candidate should not need reminding of, but use your judgement and be prepared to offer gentle advice if you think it might be necessary:

- *Never go to an interview smelling of alcohol or smoke.* Obvious.
- *Do not disparage your past employer or job* – it can never lead anywhere positive.
- *Body language* – don't contort your body, wave your limbs around, speak into your chest or avoid eye contact. Similarly, don't stare. People do strange things when they are nervous, and you should pick up on any negative body language in your own interview with the candidate. If you do, do them a favour and tell them – they may not be aware of the impression they are creating.
- *Don't be negative or talk over the interviewer* – don't be too pally either, you don't know them yet. Respect their position.

The Job

This is a must. At the very least the candidate should have seen a full and detailed job specification. You need to go through it with them, line by line, and ask, *'How does your experience tally here? What have you done in this area that you consider a success?'* Pick five of the candidate's highlights and attributes which match aspects of the job specification and make sure that they're well-drilled in talking about them. They should be able to explain not only what they've achieved, but how they achieved it. It's also vital that you give them a copy of the CV that you've sent to the client. If you've re-arranged, or highlighted, parts of the CV that the candidate gave to you then they need to know what changes you've made, and why.

Candidate Interview History

The Limitless Recruiter will drill down to find out how the candidate has performed previously in interviews. If they've had fifty job interviews in the past two years, there's a good chance that there is something about the way they are presenting themselves that isn't helping them in a face-to-face situation. You need to know about this so that you can offer advice.

If they've never had an interview before then you need to prepare them for what to expect, so that they're not overwhelmed by the experience. Tell them what kind of questions to expect – the kind your client typically asks. Also give them an idea of the personality types that have been placed at that company previously.

'The first part of your candidate preparation, as the Limitless Recruiter, is to minimalise the reasons why a client might take against them within the first minute of the interview.' – James Kingston

---

The Interview

Here are some other behaviour tips to prep your candidate with for their actual meeting with the client:

- *Be yourself* – natural behaviour is always more impressive
- *Give a firm handshake* – but don't grip for too long or yank the client's hand
- *Accept a drink* – of water (keep it simple)
- *Answer the questions asked* – not the ones you would like to have been asked
- *Allow the interviewer to guide the meeting* – don't interrupt or keep steering the subject
- *Avoid negativity* – the client will imagine you being negative in their workplace
- *Take notes* – especially if there is a point you want to follow up on
- *Ask questions at the close* – your candidate should always have questions prepared, or they risk sounding uninterested.

DEBRIEFING CANDIDATES

After the interview, you should always call the candidate before you call the client. There are two reasons for this. Firstly, if for any reason the interview has not gone well, at least you'll be prepared when you speak to the client. By contrast, the second reason is that, if it's gone really well, then you can discuss a potential offer ahead of the client contacting you to offer them the job, or possible times for a second interview – let's not get ahead of ourselves here! The point is, whether it's an egg on face or a champagne moment, debriefing the candidate first puts you in the strongest possible position. Post interview, you need to consult with your candidate to get the answers to these three crucial questions:

- *How did the interview go?*
- *Do you want the job?*
- *If offered, will you accept it?*

You can do this by debriefing the candidate with a longer series of questions, including the following:

- *'How long did the interview last?'* Although interviews can last anywhere between 15 minutes and three hours, in my experience every minute past an hour is usually a good sign.
- *'How did you get on with interviewer?'* This is important, as they are likely to be the person your candidate will be working with.
- *'Were you introduced to anyone else?'* Often, if the interview has gone well, the client will introduce the candidate to some key people.
- *'Was a second interview mentioned?'* It's amazing what a post-interview candidate may forget until you prompt them.

- *'Did the subject of money come up?'* Some people feel uncomfortable talking about money in an interview situation – clients and candidates – but for others, it's natural. Some clients like to see how a candidate will react in such a situation, especially if the job they've applied for involves managing budgets and negotiating terms on the client's behalf.
- *'What kind of future can you see for yourself at the company?'* If it's gone well, you want the candidate to be keen to take the job, so you want to reinforce their good impressions of the person they've met and the company they might be working for.
- *'What did you like about them?'* The Limitless Recruiter will take this a stage further, naturally. For every good thing the candidate says about the company you mirror it with another positive, and then keep going back and forth until they can't think of anything more. Then ask, *'Is there anything you didn't like about it?'* And no matter what they say, you don't add anything to their tally. Just keep quiet. Again, this reinforces their positive impressions.
- *'If an offer was made, what would you like it to look like?'* Get the candidate to think about a good outcome, and not just in monetary terms.
- *'How did you leave it with the interviewer?'* It's surprising how often the interviewer and interviewee have different takes on how the interview was concluded.
- *'What else are you doing about another job?'* You need to know not only if they're in the running for something else, but also how their priorities stand after this interview.
- *'Would you take the job, if offered?'* The million-dollar question.

- *'What is the bottom line that you would accept? Obviously a lower offer is not in our interests, because our fee is percentage-based, but we need to know when negotiating on your behalf.'*
- *'How would you feel if you didn't get it?'* The reaction to this question will tell you how much they really want the job, and how much flexibility they might show if the offer comes in under expectations.
- *How did you feel when you walked out the door?* If their reaction to this is really positive, then you can remind them of this later on, in the resignation process for instance.

This is also a great opportunity for you to enhance the client's reputation even more than you have done while prepping the candidate: *'Why did you like the company? Why would you want to work there? Tell me three things that you liked about this client?'* This is all great information to feed back to the client but – and this is almost equally good – it reinforces the reasons in the candidate's subconscious as to why they might want to work there.

Finally, requalify their original motivations and their expectations, as established at interview. Leave them in a positive place and hopeful. A surprising number of candidates who don't think they want the job after an interview change their minds when reminded why they were attracted to it in the first place.

DEBRIEFING CLIENTS

You've called the candidate and got their feedback – let's assume it's great. Now you need to speak to the client. Your aim in the client debrief is to find out the following:

THE ART OF RECRUITMENT

- *Can the candidate do the job?*
- *Does the client want them to do the job?*
- *Would they like to offer or second interview the candidate?*

Prompt the client with a series of well-thought-out questions. Listen to their feedback before giving any feedback from the candidate. If the client took an immediate and strong dislike to the candidate, it's better that you don't go on to argue too strongly on the candidate's behalf – you'll be damaging your future relationship with the client. Thankfully this is a rare occurrence, but you must really listen not only to what the client says at this point, but also to how they say it. Here are some of the things you might want to ask:

- *'How did it go?'* A nice open question to start with. Let the client take the lead and see where they go.
- *'Do you feel the candidate can handle the position?'* This is different from whether they *want* to employ them – it's about how they view the candidate's competence.
- *'What is it you liked about them? What made them stand out?'* Again, emphasise the strengths and play down the weaknesses. Reinforce the candidate's good points and don't react to any criticisms of them – encourage the client to see the candidate in the best possible light – reward them when they do so by reinforcing their positive impressions.
- *'What is it about their personality that would fit best within your company?'* This is a very effective leading question – it gets the client to visualize them as a member of the team already.

- *Now give an overview of the candidate's feedback* – tailored to the client's previous answers. The key, like a good sales call, is to obtain as much information as you can before giving any answers yourself. Then provide an overview of the candidate's feedback – always emphasise the positives from the candidate debrief – *'John felt exactly the same way.'* Make the client feel valued.
- *How would you like to proceed from here?* This is also the stage where you can start to introduce a sense of urgency and create desire – *'Just so you know, John has three other interviews this week and I think he's about to receive an offer from an interview he did last week. I understand you've got three other candidates to see, but if you feel he was a strong candidate it might be worth getting him in for the second interview a bit earlier.'*
- *Reconfirm the next steps* – *'Is the next interview an offering interview? If not, at what stage will you be making an offer?'* – the candidate will want to know.
- *Reconfirm the package required for the candidate to accept the job* – a lot of consultants don't discuss money until after a third interview, when an offer is put on the table that is miles below the candidate's bottom line. If the candidate's expectation is £60,000 and the client offers £30,000, it's not going to work. This happens much more than it should. If you get into a situation where the offer has to be changed more than once, with the candidate's knowledge, then it will generally fall apart. If you're negotiating on behalf of the candidate but they're not aware of the process, there's a much higher chance of success. This is where you earn your money as a consultant. You need to be able to step in and

politely but firmly guide the client – *'If you want this candidate to fill your vacancy, this is what it's going to take.'*

- *Then you establish a course of action* – the Limitless Recruiter will step in and manage this process, particularly when there is a disparity between expectations on both sides. I remember a situation where a senior management figure in a large organisation was keen to move to a smaller company because he would have more autonomy and influence in their future direction and growth. The problem was, they couldn't offer a package commensurate with what he was on, or even close, even though I had made it clear what his expectations were. They were still keen for him to join them, so I suggested that they take him out for lunch with their management team, so he could see the enthusiasm and dedication of this young company. It hadn't occurred to them to do this. He was swayed by their energy and they found a middle ground they could agree on. Do everything in your power to bring the two sides together, without making it too obvious. Always look for the positive. It won't work in every situation, but it will work better than if you do nothing but repeat parrot fashion what each side is saying to the other.
- *Requalify the client's original specifications and requirements established when the vacancy is taken* – *'You told me you wanted this, this and this. She ticks all the boxes. What you asked me for is what you've got – offer her the job!'*

OFFER PRESENTATION AND NEGOTIATION

You've got to the point of offer – the moment where you can mess it up or secure the deal. You want the candidate to come away feeling really excited, happy and saying, *'yes!'*

Before this, as soon as you hear the offer from the client, you should know in an instant whether the candidate is going to accept it or not.

Managing the Transition

Congratulations. Your candidate has been well-prepped, given a brilliant interview, presentation and second interview. She has been offered and accepted the package that you negotiated on her behalf. Job done? Not quite. You still have to manage the transition stage – this is one of the most delicate points in the recruitment process and things can very easily fall apart unless you're on top of them at all times.

The Limitless Recruiter will constantly be understanding, questioning and testing the motives of someone leaving their job for another. It's important to recognise that things rarely stay the same in people's lives and careers. It's possible your candidate's original reasons for leaving might change. For instance, they might have been worried about the financial stability of the company and then suddenly they have a new investor – everything's different. You need to be aware of this because then you can influence the process with the candidate and the client.

The general rule is that if a candidate isn't doing what you want them to do when you want them to do it – at any stage during the process – then that's a warning sign. If people have gone through the whole process – if you keep asking same questions about why they want to leave and getting the same answer – then you can be reasonably sure things are all right.

You want the candidate to be happy.

Now it's important to say that this is not the same as influencing or pressurising someone into doing something they don't want to do. Our role as consultants is to get our candidate a better job and improve their life. But there are often some obstacles along the way. A good analogy is someone who has been in an unhappy relationship for fifteen years. It's still very hard to part company with someone you've known that long, whether it's the right thing for you to do or not. The emotional attachment is strong and sometimes people need a bit of a helping hand. It's the same with jobs. They might miss out on the opportunity to leave and go on to something better because they feel intimidated by the prospect.

On a personal level, I left a job where I was at director level on a six-figure salary to go and start out on my own. It was nerve-wracking, but it was the best thing I ever did. A good consultant can relay the experiences of candidates who have faced the same dilemma – even in the same company – as reassurance and motivation to make the jump.

You can remove a lot of the fear from the transition by reiterating the reasons the candidate gave for leaving. If you do this at least four times during the recruitment process – during the candidate call, during the candidate interview preparation, as part of the candidate debrief and at the resignation – you're giving yourself the highest chance of success in placing that candidate and minimising the risk of a dropout.

RESIGNATION BRIEFING

A lot of the preparation for managing the resignation process will have been done at the candidate interview stage (by the Limitless Recruiter, at least). This will include finding out:

- *The candidate's level of relationship with their manager* – how much trust and respect is there? Is the manager's behaviour a motivator to leave, or have they always enjoyed a good relationship? You need to know so that you can frame an offer, when it comes, in the right way. *'I know it'll be a wrench to leave because you'll feel you're letting down X, but in truth you've been an exemplary employee and I'm sure she'll be pleased that you're taking this opportunity to progress.'*
- *The company procedure for resignations* – what has happened in the past when colleagues have resigned? How long does it usually take?
- *What their contractual notice period is* – then you can plan requalifying calls at regular intervals.
- *The candidate's reasons for leaving* – If their employer could resolve those reasons, would they stay? The reason we need to establish this is because it happens so often. Why? In a candidate-led market, in particular, companies never want to lose good staff – ever. Nothing makes me sadder myself. During my time as a Managing Director, we've only lost one person who I didn't want

to go. The costs – in time and money – of having to replace a valuable employee are considerable. Companies will do whatever they can to keep their top employees, so you need to be prepared to be proactive.

Buy-Backs

If you've done that preparation at interview stage, then you'll be better placed to deal with the dreaded buy-back when it occurs. Firstly, you should have pre-warned the candidate that they might well be counter-offered, should they be offered and accept a job you are putting them forward for.

Buy-back is the process of a counter-offer being made by a candidate's employer, usually shortly after the candidate has proffered their resignation. The employer will offer a salary increase, or some improvement to the candidate's terms and conditions, in order to persuade them to stay.

If you find out your candidate has been made a counter-offer don't panic, there are things you can and should say:

- *Remind them of their misgivings with their current situation –* you're not being underhand. It's just a fact that many people will suddenly see their current situation as 'safe' and the next challenge as an unknown, and cling onto the comfort blanket, even if it smells a bit and has a few stains. Remind them that they needed to resign in order to be offered a pay rise.

- *Offer positive reinforcement – 'Fast-forward five years from now – where could you be in your new company? What excites you more?'* Sometimes the transition process can take weeks or months, so strong emotional reactions experienced get blurred or forgotten – it never hurts to remind the candidate of how pleased and excited they were to be offered the position.
- *Make them think about the future if they accept a counter-offer and don't move on* – point out that a salary increase is only an advance against future pay rises and salary was only one of the reasons they gave for leaving anyway – what about the others? Will they ever be trusted again, or will they be marked out as a disloyal employee?
- *80 per cent of employees who accept a counter-offer move on within six months (according to statistics compiled by the National Employment Association).*

THE LIMITLESS RECRUITER WILL...
- **Not leave candidate interview prep to the last minute**
- **Always go the extra mile in digging down to find out about a candidate's special achievements**
- **Drill down to find out how the candidate has performed previously in interviews**
- **Make sure that both parties know all the facts and details necessary to secure the candidate and secure the position**
- **Prep the candidate so well that they've practically got the job before they walk in the door**
- **Reinforce a client's positive impressions of a candidate, but**

not their negative ones
- Always be looking at the recruitment process and think, *What can I do to influence it to my benefit and success?*

PART THREE:
RECRUITING WITHOUT LIMITS

Chapter Seven:
The DNA of a Limitless Recruiter

So far, we've looked at the recruitment industry and the process of recruitment itself. Now we're going to take it up a gear and look at the DNA of the most successful recruiters. What makes them exceptional and how do they do what they do – what is the secret to becoming a Limitless Recruiter?

How is it that two consultants, with the exact same training and knowledge, can end up having completely different careers?

In my recruitment career to date, I've worked with hundreds of consultants and interviewed thousands, and I would say that only a handful have had what it takes to be described as a Limitless Recruiter.

Back in 2002, when I first started in recruitment, I was sent off to Southampton for two weeks of introductory training to the industry with eight others in my class. Nearly twenty years on, I'm the only one of that class who, in the opinion of others, has 'made it'.

But why?

As a director and a born problem-solver, I wanted more than just to be great at recruitment myself. I wanted to know what the recipe is for a Limitless Recruiter – how to create the Michelin star chef who excels, despite being given the same ingredients as everyone else. So let's roll up our sleeves and break a few eggs…

'A Limitless Recruiter has the perfect combination of a growth mindset and a tremendous work ethic. They excel in their knowledge of the industry and in building relationships with clients and candidates. They consistently improve their performance through strategic planning and multiple goal setting. Because of their application and time management, the only limit to their success is the scope of their ambition.' – James Kingston.

As a Limitless Recruiter, I was always the top biller in every company I worked for. One of the challenges I had, when I came to take my first steps into management, was that I found it difficult to understand why everyone else wasn't operating the same way as me – and wasn't able to deliver the same results.

I started analysing my performance to try to understand why it stood out. But not just me. I've worked with some of the best consultants in the industry – both as colleagues and as competitors (Mrs. K. especially) – and I've always been curious as to what they do differently. What motivates them to achieve the success they do? So I asked them: clients, candidates, and other recruiters as well.

All the time I wanted to know the same things. From clients – *'Why are you using xxx instead of us?'* From candidates – *'What did you like about that consultant's approach better than mine?'* From competitors – *'How are you getting more business with that client than we are? What are you doing that we aren't?'* From myself, constantly – *What can I do differently to improve my performance even further?* I suggest you do the same when you meet someone whose work you respect, and whose success you would like to emulate professionally.

The obvious way of measuring success in recruitment is by placements and revenue produced – they are the two outputs that every recruiter has in common. Succeeding in this way means learning about your market and your sector, then starting to produce results, then delivering results consistently, month in, month out. That is one way to measure success. But that's not all there is to it. You might just get lucky for a while, or the market might favour the sector you're in.

After reflecting on what had made me successful – and asking other leading recruiters what they put their achievements down to – I noticed certain patterns emerging. Attributes came up time and time again with reference to the most outstanding consultants.

This was my conclusion: there are six strands which make up the DNA of a Limitless Recruiter. Each strand, or trait, is important in its own right, but it is only when they are all twisted together that the real power of the Limitless Recruiter becomes apparent.

THE SIX DNA STRANDS OF A LIMITLESS RECRUITER

Mindset

Every Limitless Recruiter has a growth mindset and will always change setbacks into positives. They constantly visualise success and adopt a 'can-do', winning attitude. The Limitless Recruiter never gives up and – when faced with a setback – asks, *'What can*

I do to make this work?' Their glass is always half-full. 'Always focused on [their] next win,' as Warren Buffett says. This is the key attribute possessed by every single successful recruiter I've ever met – the quality that sets them apart from the average. We'll look at mindset in more depth in the next chapter.

Goals, Strategy and Planning

My dad was sometimes called a dawdler, he did everything at his own pace, when he was ready. We even joked that he had his own time zone – a bit like the Tim Robbins character in *The Shawshank Redemption* who was described as 'like a man in a park without a care or a worry in the world'.

You would never say that about a Limitless Recruiter. They have a constant sense of purpose. They are on a mission. Always having short-, medium- and long-term objectives, and the strategy and tactics to achieve them, are also essential characteristics – ones that we'll discuss in more detail in Chapter 9.

The Limitless Recruiter sets goals and plans – consistently and relentlessly. They are organised and always working towards something, always looking for forward momentum. People in the recruitment industry who are truly motivated don't come up for air – they're too busy working to achieve their next goal or objective. Which brings me onto the next DNA strand:

'Be humble. Be hungry. And always be the hardest worker in the room.' – Dwayne 'The Rock' Johnson

---

THE ART OF RECRUITMENT

Work Ethic

Being a Limitless Recruiter starts and ends with your work ethic. No-one ever became great at anything by just doing the bare minimum. Going above and beyond will get you there quicker and, in recruitment terms, will fill more jobs faster. If you ask anyone who has achieved success in their profession – whether it's a Premier League footballer, a film star, an entrepreneur or a recruitment consultant – they will tell you their secret is hard work. This is not news. I think we're all aware that 'what you put in is what you get out.' But it's one thing to acknowledge this truth and another to follow through.

Think of it this way. If you were a fly on the wall of your office watching yourself, how much of the working day are you honestly productive? How much of the day are you actually 'on it'? The most successful recruiters are always working. They're not sitting back watching the cricket on the corner of their PC, or playing games on their phones, texting their partner, or scrolling through social media. They are 'on it' for every minute of their working day. When they are in the office, nothing breaks their concentration to be the best, do the best and achieve the most in the time allocated to their job. Always working harder than everyone else is what produces results.

'If you want somethin', go get it. Period.' – Chris Gardner (Will Smith) in The Pursuit of Happyness.'

I have always worked every minute I have available to me. At any given moment I am mastering focus, avoiding distractions and always doing something that is taking me closer to achieving my goals more quickly and more often than others.

At my peak, as a temporary white-collar consultant, I was producing a turnover of over £5 million annually, with a gross margin of £400 –500k. This did not happen by accident. Working twelve-hour days, I was always on the phone or on visits, constantly working towards filling roles and marketing out candidates.

But just working hard is never enough, just like having great plans, goals and strategies isn't enough. You need both. My life has got busier and busier as I've become more successful, but I still plan every single day and know what I want to have achieved by the time I'm ready to go home. Some excellent recruiters are 9–5 people. Not me. I have always been the first in and last out in the office and, even when I'm not at work, I'm working. That's in my DNA and there is an argument that says most people who truly succeed in recruitment, and in life, consistently break personal bests – they aren't 9–5 people. They go above and beyond for themselves and for others. Like David Beckham staying behind after training to practice free kicks for hours, they are always looking for ways to improve themselves and their performance. In black and white terms, the more calls you make and the greater your level of activity, the better you will get and the more likely you are to succeed. Working hard and smart is how you become a Limitless Recruiter.

THE ART OF RECRUITMENT

Relationships

People buy from people. If you know your market and you can deliver, that's great, but what if your competitors can too? What makes the difference between a good, run-of-the-mill consultant and a Limitless Recruiter? *Relationships.*

If you ever attend an international sporting event, look at the VIP boxes. Who is in them? Probably a member of the royal family and a few well-known celebrities, but they'll be outnumbered by clients of corporate hospitality.

Why are VIP boxes such a popular fixture at sporting and cultural events? Because companies realise the importance of looking after your established clients and building relationships with new ones. The Limitless Recruiter has such good relationships with clients that he goes to their weddings and attends other social occasions with them. Situations which extend beyond business transactions. They like their clients. Their clients like them. They are regularly in contact talking about aspects of daily life other than recruitment. Having a bit of fun, sharing personal moments.

As I've suggested elsewhere, if you can *really* get to know your clients – their pet hates and passions – not only does it make your professional relationship easier, but it puts you in a better position to recruit the kind of people who are going to fit in around them.

Recruitment stopped being 'a job' for me after my second year – I loved going out to meet clients, having a chat and getting to know them better. I love getting the recipe right, I love great recruitment and I have a genuine passion for people. People who don't bother with this aspect of recruitment reach a certain level, perhaps, but they'll never go further.

These relationships enable repeat and often exclusive business, introductions to new clients and they will make the difference if you are in a bun fight with another recruiter over who sent a CV first!

The best recruiters are the ones who know about vacancies before the Preferred Supplier List (PSL) agencies, who are discussing the client's next project and future roles, and who, ultimately, are the first people the client thinks of when looking to hire new staff – a partner, not a supplier.

Relationships start with honesty, integrity and trust. I have clients who will give me every CV they receive from other recruiters to make us aware of who's on the market – our relationship is that strong. I have one client who I'd arranged to meet one morning. I walked into his office and he had a stack of 90 CVs on his desk. He pointed to it and sighed, *'Look, I need ten good candidates from this pile. I haven't got the time to go through all that, could you sort it for me?'*

That's the kind of trust and mutual respect you want to build towards. It won't happen overnight, but with patience these things develop naturally. If a client thinks they can trust you and your opinions then you're halfway there. And why would they do that? Because you've consistently shown yourself to be professional and trustworthy. No shortcuts, no bullshit. If you take away one lesson from this chapter, let it be that acting with integrity will earn you respect from your colleagues, candidates and clients.

Building relationships takes time, but there are things you can do to create great relations with your clients that will kick other recruiters to the kerb and make sure you get every single bit of business.

No one ever remembers *Joe Average*, people always remember the extremes – very good and very bad. The former will keep you in their good graces. The latter will close a door and it's very hard (though not impossible) to rebuild a relationship that's been broken.

Let me give you a couple of examples which might entertain you, if nothing else! If you were a client and a recruiter you didn't know very well offered you drugs at a Christmas lunch, how would you feel? Respected? If, on the other hand, you were a temp and your consultant paid your salary out of his own wages one week – because he'd promised you work, but the client had pulled the job at the last moment – well, I hope you'd feel a bit of loyalty. And if you were the client who pulled the job and got to hear about what this consultant had done – might you also feel a bit of respect and also loyalty to that person? Both true examples, by the way.

So, what can you do that other recruiters don't? Think outside the box and think what would add value to your client. Demonstrate that you care about more than just offering a service. Nominate a client for an award, for instance, send them a lead for business, or an email about a relevant article you've read about them in the media. You could show a public display of affection for their company on social media, donate to their charity fundraiser or – even better – help them with an event they are organising.

Getting to know clients personally is the key to a long-lasting, exclusive relationship. The only way to truly build the strongest bridges is to take them out of the office environment. Invite them for a drink, a meal, a social event – corporate hospitality, if your company allows it – if they don't, or they don't see the benefit, you're with the wrong company! Guards are down at these events. You will get to know the client better and they won't just see you as a money-hungry, 'typical recruitment consultant', who's only after one thing. Going the extra mile, in relationship development, is a sure-fire way to build bonds with clients that will take your relationship above and beyond all other recruiters.

Knowledge

The Limitless Recruiter knows every single company in their area: they know the challenges that they face, their supply chain and business networks, and what's going on in the wider industry. Having this knowledge is vital to being seen and heard in your sector. Having your finger on the pulse puts you in pole position to act first and reflects a growth mindset. You know what else? It makes your life more interesting too.

It's not just that you're showing a willingness to learn about what the client does, but you should feel that you *must* know more because it will help you deliver a better service. Any successful recruiter will tell you there is no prize for coming second on a deal. Increasing and updating your knowledge should be one of your key tactics in implementing a successful client management strategy. As my old MD used to say,

'Knowledge is power, and everyone wants to know everyone else's business. Master the gossip and you'll be the first they call.'

Taking it to the next level, the Limitless Recruiter will find that they actually add value to the client's business. For instance, I have given clients leads which help them to win more work. Because we do business and build relationships with the clients of clients, we can offer feedback when opportunities arise for our clients – which we are often the first to hear about. Who do you think such a client is going to ask to handle their additional recruitment needs in this scenario?

This kind of approach may not apply in every recruitment sector, but always be looking for opportunities to increase your knowledge about an important client's business. Knowing what's happening in their industry makes you more appealing to a client. It doesn't look as though you're only interested in them for one thing if you are genuinely engaged in their world and how it operates. I've got a client who rings me every fortnight and asks, *'What's going on? What's the latest gossip?'* Knowledge is a resource like any other – acquire it and use it.

When a client's competitor is about to go under, you will know all the key staff who are going to be made redundant – that is gold dust. Blink, and the moment has gone; another faster, quicker and slicker recruiter has already contacted them. Or a client has just been awarded a project but it's not out in the open yet, but you know because you are friends with the Awards PR Manager. I once told a client they had won a job before they even knew themselves – massive brownie points for me, and guess who had the project director placed on the job, before it was even on anyone's radar?

Challenging and Questioning Everything

Often not making a placement or not getting a vacancy results from being afraid or reluctant to ask the right question at the right time. Sometimes these may be tough questions, to which you might not like the answers. The Limitless Recruiter is not afraid to challenge anyone or any situation if he or she thinks it is necessary.

Challenging the status quo is often the only way to determine whether you need to try a different approach or a different activity in any given situation. Prying more, digging deeper to ensure everything is moving the way you want it to. Why? Why not? Let me give you an example from my own experience. It's one that's not uncommon to recruitment.

I had a client who offered a starting salary of £68,000 to a candidate who was on £65,000. It wasn't a bad offer but, because of my knowledge of the candidate's company, I knew that his previous boss had just lost two staff and so was likely to do anything in his power to get him to stay. I also knew my candidate was nervous about making the move, despite the very real career progression it would give him. I challenged the client and said my hunch was the offer needed to be £72,500 to make certain. Because we had a good relationship and he trusted me, he took my advice. Sure enough, the candidate was counter-offered £75k but £72.5k with the good career opportunity was enough to persuade him to proceed.

Not accepting the status quo and not just hoping for the best has been crucial to my career success. It has paid dividends. I've had a success rate of four out of five for all the interviews I've arranged. So out of every five interviews, four people got the jobs and four fees were paid to my agency. Having foresight and being prepared to challenge is so important. Drilling down into the detail of *what if, what if, what if*, then challenging the client by saying, *'If you don't do this then you're not going to get the candidate'*.

So, don't be afraid to say to the client, *'OK that's fantastic, thanks for giving me these vacancies to fill but what are they dependent on? If we get you candidates, when will you be able to see them? What could jeopardise the process? What if I spend a month working on all these roles and you don't come back to me? If they are that important would you consider a retainer, so that at least my time is covered?'*

Imagine you've asked a new candidate to send you their CV and they haven't, then you have to chase them for it, then you arrange an interview for them in a temp job the following Monday. You haven't been able to reference them for one reason or another. Should you cross your fingers and hope that everything will work out? They looked good on the CV you finally received from them last thing on Friday. No. Challenge them! Say, *'Can I trust you to turn up? What guarantee can you give me that you'll be there?'* Don't bury your head in the sand and hope for the best. Cover every angle – every possibility – and always have a back-up plan!

Again, acquiring the confidence to challenge in this way doesn't happen overnight. It's a real sign of maturity and often comes from mistakes learnt. When I see consultants start to behave in this way, I know they're learning from experience and they have a growth mindset. They are demanding more information from every part of the process – not just going through the motions on autopilot.

A Limitless Recruiter will challenge every part of the process to make sure every part of the process gets a result. Taking every opportunity to increase productivity.

From time to time I hear consultants saying, when an offer comes in for one of their candidates, *'Oh, he's not going to take that anyway. No way.'* I only hear them say it once, because I challenge them on their thinking. I ask, *'What was the point of going through the whole recruitment process to that point and then throwing all that hard work and effort away because you couldn't be bothered to challenge the offer, or your candidate's assumptions?'* It's the kind of thing that only someone who isn't seeing the bigger picture will say. They shouldn't be resigned to an outcome. It just shows that they haven't drilled down enough, that they've ignored warning signs, that they've been wasting their time – which to my mind is the biggest crime a recruiter can commit.

I always have a rule when it comes to getting an outcome I want. I ask myself a set of questions. Firstly, what is the percentage chance that this likely to go my way? If I only had £1,000 left in my bank account, how much would I put down as a bet this will work? If the answers to either of these questions are low then I need to plan for my back up. So many recruiters just hope for one possible outcome and wait until it's too late to control the situation.

It all goes back to relationship building and time management. The Limitless Recruiter will always be time efficient and get results.

These six strands working together form the DNA make-up of the best recruiters in the industry. If you always keep them in mind, ensure you consistently focus on each and every area – and what you can do to strengthen the bonds between them – then you will be on your way to becoming a Limitless Recruiter yourself.

THE LIMITLESS RECRUITER WILL...

- **Have a growth mindset and always change setbacks into positives**
- **Set goals and plans – consistently and relentlessly**
- **Be 'on it' for every minute of their working day**
- **Create great relationships with their clients**
- **Have their finger on the pulse and know what's going on in the wider industry**
- **Challenge and question everything.**

Chapter Eight:
Becoming a Limitless Recruiter
– Motivation, Mindset and
Environment

'It ain't about how hard ya hit. It's about how hard you can get hit and keep moving forward.' – Rocky Balboa (Sylvester Stallone).

This chapter is about you. Specifically, it's about preparing you to succeed in recruitment – to become a Limitless Recruiter. Before we get on to specific advice that will improve your performance in every area of recruitment, we need to make sure that you are at your most receptive and that you're finely-tuned – like a thoroughbred, a Formula One driver, or a world class athlete. I want to put you in pole position to succeed in your chosen profession. We need to be sure that your motivation and your mindset – and the environment in which you live and work – are enabling you to be the best recruiter you can be.

If you're about to run a marathon, box in a title fight or take part in any type of competition, you want to be at peak performance – you need to know you can perform at your best to ensure you will win. Otherwise, the consequences could be disastrous. Why would you think any differently about your job? About recruitment?

In the next chapter I'll provide the tools which will enable you to put the theory into practice and encourage you to analyse yourself, set the right goals and have an iron-clad plan so you can achieve them. This chapter is all about ensuring that you stand out. That you're the best you can possibly be at your job. It's advice from someone who's been there, seen it, done it – me. It's amazing what a couple of tweaks to your mindset and lifestyle can make to your day-to-day performance. It's the difference between being ordinary and being exceptional. *Dig deeper to get further.*

MOTIVATION

'Motivation is one of those words that's used constantly, but few know what it really means. Motivation is not just about having the energy you need to get through your daily to-do list. It's the internal process that incites action for you to move toward a certain goal.' – Tony Robbins

---

One of the first questions I ask recruiters and candidates is, *'Do you know what motivates you?'* Most recruiters say 'money', but the answer is rarely that simple. Motivation is like starting the engine of your car and beginning to move off. What gets you leaping out of bed on a wet, cold February morning? Nothing? I bet there is something. Everyone has different motivations, and different levels of motivation. What may seem like a simple question is actually a bit more complicated when you drill down. It's essential that you understand what drives you, though, because without that knowledge you'll never truly be able to achieve your goals.

Why are you in recruitment – what objectives do you have?

If you could fast forward five years from now and you were a success, what would that look like? Would you be working in the same offices, with the same colleagues? Would you be their boss? Perhaps you'd be somewhere else, in your own offices, with a completely new team of people. Would you be living in a penthouse, in a prestigious postcode area, or would you have a big house with a large garden for your growing family, somewhere further out? Maybe you're on a beach with a laptop, working two hours a day and loving the balance. What sort of car is this successful version of you driving, or do you not much care? Are you more concerned with how much money you have stashed in your pension, so you can aim for an early retirement?

Drilling down into what you really want isn't always easy. As I've said, most people will say they're motivated by money, but if I ask them, *'Why?'* it turns out that's not strictly true. *'What would you spend your money on?' 'How much money, precisely, is success to you?'* are questions which elicit more interesting answers. Money isn't happiness. It's what we do with it, and what we want to do with it, that determines what gives us satisfaction – and that answer will vary from person to person. So, what you should be asking yourself is, *'If I earned £1 million, what would I spend it on? What would excite me? And what moments do I want to experience in the future?'*

Write down your answers – they might determine what you want to get out of your career. As a bonus, without realising it, you've just created your bucket list. Keep your answers close, as we shall be using them in the next chapter when we look at how to use your motivation and personal milestones to set the right goals.

And, by the way, just by buying this book and reading this far, you're showing me that you have a certain mindset – that you're hungry for self-improvement. In fact, you have a similar mindset to me, in that you're motivated to win.

Motivation and Needs

We are all motivated by our needs. Psychologists, like Abraham Maslow (look him up), have studied how humans are behaviourally motivated. Without boring you with the details, his theory was that people's motivations begin with a base level of *Survival Needs* – food, water, warmth and rest – and then move up a series of levels, to the highest, which he defined as *Self-Actualization*.

So, once survival needs have been met, people are then motivated to achieve their *Safety Needs* – such as emotional and financial security. From there, the individual will seek to fulfil their *Interpersonal Needs* through friendships and relationships, and so on. This scale – known as 'Maslow's hierarchy of needs' – is still widely used and referred to in management training and sociology.

Many people consider that it's not necessarily the case that all the needs at one level must be met before the individual moves to the next level, or that there may be some overlap and back-tracking as circumstances change. It is, however, a very useful tool for self-analysis and career development.

'So,' I hear you ask, 'What's this got to do with me? Or my recruitment career?' The answer is *everything*. I thoroughly recommend that you give this some serious thought. Consider how your needs are being fulfilled.

Your survival needs are most likely being met. If you're not getting enough warmth, water and food you probably won't be reading this (though you might be burning it to keep you warm).

Moving up to safety needs, however, may give you more pause for thought. Here, 'safety' covers a wide range of needs, like emotional and financial security, as well as health and well-being. Take a minute to list how the absence of these things might affect your drive and your performance at work. If your finances are on the edge, your housing is insecure and your job at risk, it's not necessarily going to help you perform at your best, is it? You'll be distracted, worried and unfocused.

I'm not saying you should use these factors as excuses, but realising that outside pressures impact on our mental well-being is very useful. Understanding something involves ceasing to be afraid of it, because once you've identified a problem you can solve it. If your rent is too high and it is worrying you to the point where you can't sleep, you're going to be less productive in the office. Think about moving somewhere that allows you to start saving and enjoying your time off more.

And so on. Having a strong network of family support and close friends has obvious benefits. Connections with people help you to fight off feelings of anxiety and loneliness, which can affect anyone at any time. Good friends help bolster your self-esteem, too. Everyone wants to feel significant, unique – appreciated for being who they are. These things are sometimes taken for granted, but never should be. For instance, I've seen seemingly unstoppable, loud extrovert candidates crumble when they move to a new job in a different area, because they've left their support network behind. Some people thrive on a feeling of independence – living in a big city on their own – but others don't. One situation isn't better or more admirable than the other. You owe it to yourself to assess honestly what works best for you and plan your career moves accordingly. You should also be thinking about these factors when drilling down to uncover your candidates' motivations.

Finally, when your needs in the areas of survival, safety, self-esteem, love and friendship are all being met to some degree, it brings you closer to *Self-Actualization*. This is the ability to become the best that one can be and fulfil your potential – in your work and personal life. Tony Robbins, the world-renowned author, life coach and motivational speaker, refers to this need as 'growth', which will unleash the power from within yourself. When you've realised your more basic needs – in terms of security, connections and significance – you can look more outwards for fulfilment, making a contribution to your workplace and to the wider community. That's what we want for you in recruitment, and outside work too.

We'll look in more depth at the practical ways you can measure your needs and accomplishments in the second part of this chapter. For now, the takeaway from this is for you to think beyond the goals you have. To think more about how and why these things are important to you, and what motivations underlie them.

Motivation and Goals

What motivates you will in large part determine the goals that you set for yourself – in your life and in your career. We shall look at this in more depth in Chapter 9, but before you get to the departure lounge, we need to work out where you should actually be going.

Every person who works for me has multiple goals – daily, weekly, monthly, quarterly, annually – and can see where they will fit into our long-term vision. It's very easy to have a single aim, such as *'I want to run my personal best in a race'* or, *'I want to buy a house.'* Not many people go straight from *'I want to buy a house'* to buying one though, do they? No, they plan and then achieve a series of goals: saving enough for a deposit, finding a property they like within their budget, getting a mortgage they can afford, working out how they will pay off that mortgage. Similarly, only the very stupid go from being a couch potato to running a marathon in a week. It takes time, training, and preparation – attention to diet, choosing the right gear, fitting a running schedule around your other daily activities.

It should be the same with your career. Every single person in my office – and every one of the hundreds of recruiters I've worked with – have all had different things they get out of bed for. Success is measured uniquely for every person – depending on their motivations, background, current situation and long-term goals. Once you have your goals you then need to plan a strategy and establish tactics to ensure you achieve them. I call this the goal journey. Firstly, we need to work out the destination, then map out the route to get there and then we need a few stops on the way, just to check we're not going off-piste and will arrive on time.

Rewards and Recognition

To keep yourself motivated you need rewards and recognition. Do people know what you're doing? Is your line manager or company aware of your goals? In my organisation part of our culture is to have everyone's goals written down. Each consultant emails them to me and then – every month or quarter when they've been achieved – we read them out and give the person a round of applause, and they stick their hand in the Goal Jar. At the end of the year, we all go out together and talk about the goals that have been achieved within the business. We also celebrate the little successes along the way. For a consultant's first placement, or if they break a Kingston Barnes record, they'll receive a bottle of champagne to mark the moment. It's a nice, positive thing to do – recognition is important, reward is important.

MINDSET

'The most powerful tool in my armoury is my mindset.' – *Ant Middleton*

To achieve your goals, you need a positive or growth mindset. What is a mindset? Basically, it can be defined as 'a set of attitudes that determines how you will interpret and respond to situations'.

    If I said to you,

'I've got this candidate – Joe Bloggs – I want you to get on the phone and get him five interviews today,' your first response might be to think, *No chance*. But if I said,

'I'll give you £10,000 if you get Mr Bloggs five interviews today,' do you think you would manage it? In an instant: failure is not an option. Your mind will immediately switch to, *What do I need to do to get the job done?* What has changed in that brief space of time? Have you learned more skills? No. Has Joe Bloggs become a better candidate? No. Has your mindset changed? *Yes.* I've taken the focus away from a fear of failure – and that's one of the mindsets which holds a lot of people back.

This fear of failure – a negative mindset – affects us all to varying degrees and at different times. We have to constantly guard against it. There are practices we can put in place to combat it, like creating a plan for successful change. Indeed, working on a positive mindset should become part of our routine. A habitual thing – adopting good habits and practices – is how we change our mindset when its focus is on the wrong objectives.

There are things we can do to reduce the fear, too. Ask yourself, *What's the worst that can happen?* Then think about what you need to do to ensure that it doesn't happen. Plan, prepare and visualise success. In football, and many other sports, a well-used tactic is to visualise the scoring of a goal before the opportunity to score presents itself. Visualise success and you have a higher chance of achieving it. Conversely, if you fear failure and anticipate it in an activity – if you don't believe you will succeed before you start – you probably won't. The fear of failure is like a voice in your head, instantly doubting yourself before you even try. It will infect your efforts, and ultimately the result – you're doomed to fail before you start.

So what can we do to keep that voice at bay? Matthew McConaughey says,

'We all have got two wolves in us – a good one, and a bad one. They both wanna eat. We just gotta feed that good one a little more than the other one.' So, let's feed the positive wolf in us!

Here are a couple of practices I've instigated at my company to keep the mindset positive. It's something you can do too – either for yourself, with a colleague or in your team. I ask my staff to have their biggest achievements to date written down in front of them, as a constant reminder that they've already achieved success and can do whatever they put their minds to. Also, at the end of the day, before everyone leaves the office, I get them to tell me one great thing they've achieved during that day. It doesn't have to be money on the board or a great interview – it could be that they've spoken to a promising new client or candidate, or that they've arranged a company visit. Even that they've taken a glowing reference to add to their candidate marketing call the next day. The point of the exercise is that you're leaving the office for the day on a high and then you'll come in fresh and motivated the next day.

Similarly, when you're about to do something, visualise it going the right way. Before you spec out a candidate, imagine the call going really well and the client wanting to see them. Before you make a cold call, picture the conversation being really positive and the client having a vacancy and giving it to you.

It's a bit like a first date, or a best man's speech. If you spend the whole time worrying about it going wrong, visualising it going wrong – what do you think is going to happen when the time comes? Feed the right beast!

Whenever I'm about to make a speech, or do any type of activity, I imagine it going the way I want. If I'm a keynote speaker, or have the honour of being a best man, I imagine the audience laughing with, not at me (a lesson learned from my first best man speech at the age of 24 – but let's not go there). I see the whole room being entranced by my words, keeping their attention throughout, and people truly benefitting and learning from, and enjoying the message I'm delivering. Guess what happens when I take the stand in this mindset? This is a great exercise for confidence-building too.

'Motivation and mindset affect everything.' – James Kingston

Fixed Mindset v. Growth Mindset

The late, great salesman Richard Denny once told me,

'People set their own limitations. They put up barriers because they don't believe they're good enough to achieve something. You get people who want to smash through the ceiling and then others who are happy enough to just touch it. They have different levels of expectations, which are governed by their mindset.'

We may broadly define these people as having either a growth mindset or a fixed mindset. Consider this example. I have a very competent consultant working for me. He has been billing about £10,000 a month consistently for fifteen years. I have no complaints – he is a good recruiter, represents the business well and is a team player – but I was slightly mystified because I knew he wasn't fulfilling his potential. I asked him in for a meeting and said,

'You're one of our most consistent performers.' His face lit up.

'Have we seen the best of you though?' His face fell slightly.

'What do you mean?' he asked.

'Well,' I said, '£10k a month. When did this become normal for you? Why not £20k? £30k? Even £50k?'

'Are you not happy with my performance?' he asked, looking crestfallen.

'It's not that,' I said, 'so much as I don't think you should be happy with it. You're coasting in fourth gear, doing the same things the same way – day in, day out. You're not being the best you can be – or pushing yourself to your full potential. You have a fixed mindset. Think about this. I can run a business and still bill £100k in three months. I'm not saying that you should be doing the same, but why can't you do £20k a month? I think it's because your daily activity is geared towards hitting £10k a month. You're not challenging yourself, and, eventually you'll just get stale or bored. Why don't we see what we need to do to get you to £20k a month instead?' It was a light-bulb moment for him. He could see that the only limitations on his achievements were being set by his mindset. We worked out a plan and set him some goals that would really challenge him and push him to his potential. His performance improved within months. He's a lot happier now and has more money in his pocket, too.

The brain is like a muscle – it gets stronger and functions better the more it is exercised. Unfortunately, many people believe the opposite – that the brain is static, that any talents we have are fixed, unchanging personal attributes we are born with. We are either destined for success and accomplishment or not, depending on our innate qualities. This is simply not true. You don't need to be born intelligent to be smart! Every time you work hard, challenge yourself and learn something new your brain forms new neural pathways and connectors – over time you become smarter. Carol Dweck, a Professor of Psychology at Stanford University, defined these differing outlooks:

Fixed Mindset – *intelligence is a fixed trait.*
Growth Mindset – *intelligence is a quality that can be changed and developed. (Carol Dweck, 2008)*

Consider how you approach the following scenarios:

• When a new challenge comes up – something you've never done before – what's your response? Is it positive? Is it negative? Does it get you excited or scared? How do you react?
• Have you tried to influence a negative situation to turn it into a positive one? How did you think about it and talk about it, express it?
• Do you sometimes look for reasons why you might fail, or why others have failed??

I'll be honest. I sometimes analyse a situation negatively before I look for the positives, but with a winning mindset to put it right. For instance, if a consultant comes to me with a dilemma, I might focus on the one thing they are doing wrong in the process rather than the nine things they did right, so we can focus on tweaking the process to get it perfect.

A growth mindset is the most important component of your training. It will put you in the right state of mind to achieve your goals in recruitment and in life. By reducing and removing mental obstacles and fears, you put yourself in pole position to achieve success. Let's look at this in a bit more detail.

Steps to Developing a Growth Mindset

Step #1: Learn, learn, learn

Step #2: Realise hard work is key

Step #3: Face setbacks head-on.

Mindset Step #1: Learn, learn, learn

Fixed Mindset: Look infallible at all costs – 'The main thing I want to do at work is to show others how good I am.'

Growth Mindset: Learn, learn, learn – 'It's much more important for me to learn, by asking and observing others, than to appear infallible.'

Mindset Step #2: Realise hard work is key

Fixed Mindset: Accomplishment should come naturally – 'When I have to work really hard at something, I don't feel very clever'; 'I don't need to make any more sales calls'.

Growth Mindset: Putting a lot of effort in and working hard is key – 'The harder I have to work at something, the more effort I put into something, the better I'll be at it'; 'I'll make more sales calls to maximise my opportunities.'

Mindset Step #3: Face Setbacks

Fixed Mindset: Hide mistakes and conceal deficiencies, retreat, blame others, act superior – 'I'd spend less time on this client from now on'; 'I won't put this candidate forward ever again.'

Growth Mindset: Capitalise on mistakes and confront deficiencies – 'I will work harder on my relationship with this client from now on'; 'I will strive to understand why this candidate did not get the job, and what to look for in the next person. I'll also try and market them out for a more suitable position.'

Dealing with Rejection

One of the biggest challenges to a growth mindset is dealing with rejection. Nothing makes us want to find an excuse or someone to blame for our failure more than avoiding the feeling of rejection.

In recruitment it's possible that you might (rarely) get shouted or sworn at by a client or candidate. When something bad like this happens, it may be out of your control. In recruitment you're dealing with people, not paper, and people can be unpredictable. The important thing is never to take it personally and don't give up.

You might have a couple of bad calls, a placement drop out, or a barren couple of months. If you have a fixed mindset, you might decide that it's because you're not good enough, or other people are treating you unfairly and there's nothing you can do about it.

You have to push past that barrier of negativity. Think, *What's happened? Why? Have I done everything I could? What could I do differently? What can I do to make sure it doesn't happen again? What am I going to do about it now?* Learn from the experience –

don't be ashamed to admit there was something you missed. This way you'll develop a growth mindset. If the answer is truly nothing – there is nothing you could have done to influence the situation for the better, if there is no one you could have asked for advice – then don't worry about it. Move on. That's the mindset you need.

Case Study

We did an executive search for a very senior commercial position – a six-figure salary. It took us three months to identify the right person. A hundred attempted phone calls, 80 people head-hunted specifically for the position. Eventually we whittled the list down to three excellent candidates whom we put forward for a three-stage interview process. The company made their selection. T--- looked like a perfect fit. He'd been with same company for fifteen years and he was ready for a new challenge. They agreed terms and he handed his notice in. Everything was great.

His company didn't want him to go. I had the counter-offer conversation with him – *'Why do you want to leave? How did you feel when you received the new offer? Where do you think you'll be happiest? Which position do you prefer and which do you see ticking the boxes long-term? What would be different if you stayed? Is there anything your current employer could do to change your mind?'* At the end of the process T--- was convinced he'd made the right decision.

'I'm definitely going, James, I'm really excited. My notice is in, and I can't wait to get started,' he told me. I kept in touch with him for every week of his three-month notice period. I even took him out to lunch a couple of times. There were no problems: the deal was done.

Day one – the start date – the client called me.

'James, where's T---?'

'What do you mean, "where's T---?"'

'Well, he hasn't turned up and it's his first day.'

'That's strange, give me a moment.' I checked my voicemail and emails. Nothing. I picked up the phone to T---. There was no answer. He didn't respond to emails or at his home number. I rang his previous employer's main number and got put through to him under a false pretext.

'T---, are you at the right company today?'

'James, I'm so sorry. I just didn't have the courage to tell you. I'm splitting up with my wife and everything is up in the air right now. My company has told me they're going to pay me 25 per cent more. I'm going to stay put. Sorry.'

We'd spent three months working really hard on this assignment. So, shit, okay. Think. *Had I done everything I could? Did I keep in touch with the candidate and the client throughout?* Yes. *What could I have done differently?* I went through every stage in my head. There was not a fault in the whole process – nothing. *Could I have done anything better?* No. Fine. *What can I do about it now?* I went back to original shortlist – there were two other people they had been keen on, including one candidate who was on more money than the client was offering. I called him. He had improved himself over the three months since the interview and he still really wanted the job. I put him forward to the client, stressing that they'd have to pay more to get him – if they still liked him. He came back to the table with a presentation that blew them away and he was only on a month's notice – so we ended up getting a bigger fee from the client the following month.

And the first candidate is now one of my best clients. We've placed eight candidates with him this year. Every situation can be turned around into a positive.

Like anything in life it's about taking the hits and dealing with it. You get knocked down, accept it and move forward. That's a growth mindset. *Is there anything I could I have done differently?* If yes, learn and adapt. Grow. If no, forget it and move on. Either way, take responsibility.

These are the Growth Mindset Questions you need to ask yourself in any recruitment situation that isn't going, or hasn't gone, to plan:

Growth Mindset Questions
- What has happened?
- Why has it happened?
- Have you done everything you could do?
- Is there anything else you can do?
- Can you ask for help?
- What are you going to do about it now?
- What are you going to do to prevent it happening again?

Once you've answered those questions, and taken any action required, just move on.

ENVIRONMENT

As well as your motivations and your mindset you need to consider your environment. By environment I mean factors like your physiological needs – the maintenance of your body – and the environments that you live and work in. All these things will impact on your mindset and motivations, subtly and not so subtly, as we saw briefly while considering Motivation and Needs.

I was fortunate to meet a man who knows a lot about preparing himself for challenging environments – Ross Edgley, the British adventurer and extreme athlete. Ross had not long completed a swim around the whole of Great Britain (1,780 miles), which took him 157 days to complete. He burnt off nearly 15,000 calories a day, surviving jellyfish, whirlpools and tongue rot in the process! To prepare for such a daunting physical and mental challenge, Ross applied all the available science to everything he knew would contribute to his performance. He also required rock solid self-discipline and a hell of a lot of resilience.

Whilst recruitment doesn't require quite the same intensity of demands as Ross's aquatic odyssey, the principles are the same. You're swimming in a big ocean of recruitment, competing with many other fish. You do need to make sure your environment contributes to your performance in a positive way, rather than having a negative effect on the way you think, feel and respond to events.

THE ART OF RECRUITMENT

Diet

Food

Are you eating the right kind of food to enable you to perform at your peak? Is your diet geared to your success, or do you eat dirty burgers washed down with a pint of lager for lunch? Diet and nutrition are massive subjects and there simply isn't room here to go into much detail, but it's common sense that what you eat, in and out of the office, will affect how you manage your desk during the day. The afternoon slump is a familiar feeling, brought on by the processing of a heavy lunch, but what and when you eat in the evening will also affect your sleeping patterns. Food for thought.

Drink

Now, we're in recruitment, right? Surely we all like a drink? I have celebrated some of my best moments in recruitment with a concoction of strong continental lager, Dom Pérignon, Hendrick's and slim lime, and a few shots of whatever is left behind the bar. Most of my twenties was spent enjoying a drink – whether it was a wind-down after a hard day, or just a Thursday, Friday or Saturday night. Most young recruiters live for the lifestyle. But a question you will ask yourself at some point is, *When does it stop?* And at what point does it start affecting your performance the next day?

Case in point is the biggest cautionary tale I tell every recruiter who works with me. I worked with one of the best recruiters in the business. He was, in his heyday, the go-to guy whom everybody knew as the Top Dog in the company. A legend who worked hard and played even harder! Think *The Wolf of Wall Street* and you're not far off.

Too many years hitting the booze hard, combined with some Class A drugs (some recruiters have a tendency to mix the two, believe it or not), and soon the cracks started to appear. Coming out the toilets at three in the afternoon, looking like he had been eating doughnuts, was the time I realised, *Jesus, P---- has a problem*.

Ten years on, he is out of the sector, he's lost his licence, he's single, no one will give him a job. He basically struggles to function in a way you and I would consider normal. A complete 180, and all because of abuse. Now, I'm not telling you this to scare you off completely, as no doubt we need times where we can let our hair down and just let loose.

But think of it this way, just for a second. Think about the hangovers – would you run a race with one? Would you stand at the altar on your wedding day with one? Guess how many drinks Ross Edgley had whilst he was swimming twelve hours a day? Why should it be any different when you go to work? Enjoy life, experiment even, but if you want to be truly successful then follow the old adage of 'everything in moderation'. A lesson I learned in my twenties! A glass or two won't harm anyone and is a good way to celebrate success. But if the glass becomes a habit requiring a daily bottle of wine then it's not so healthy. It's a problem for many old-school recruiters – if you're hungover every Friday morning, or feel like shit every Monday morning in the office, are you really going to perform at your best? Probably not. If you must drink, save it for Friday or Saturday, when you can enjoy your tipples guilt-free and still come in on Monday bright-eyed and bushy-tailed.

Exercise and Appearance

To be the Limitless Recruiter you need to take this seriously. Alongside diet, exercise makes a massive difference to your day-to-day performance. The benefits of regular exercise are huge and will impact your life in many positive ways, from increased energy levels and stamina, and resistance to illness, to keeping you feeling and looking your best. If you eat sensibly and exercise on a regular basis, you'll end up looking the part and feeling the part.

Dress as the person you want to be. Dress for your boss's job. How you look is a reflection of you. Consider how you judge people by their professional appearance and then think about how people might describe you to a colleague. If you could pick three things you'd like people to say about your appearance, what would they be? Set these as some of your goals. The way you live your life will eventually catch up with you. Trust me, I know. I lost both my parents in their sixties to poor choices and poor lifestyles, and it's something I'm determined to learn from. Exercising daily will make you live longer and feel better and happier. Whether it's the gym, running, yoga, squash, boxing, football – or even roller skating – just find something you enjoy that will get your heart racing and make it part of your routine.

Invest in your body as much as your mind and it will thank you for it, I promise you!

Managing Stress – Meditation

A little bit of stress can be a good thing; indeed, we need it to perform at our best. However, too much stress tips us the other way. It impedes our ability to focus and work productively. We can end up becoming a whole different character – resentful, angry and short-tempered. Long-term stress can really impact your mental and physical health. It took me years to realise my constant stomach pains (IBS) were my body's way of telling me to slow down and listen.

Over the past decade the benefits of mindfulness and meditation on business practice and performance have become widely recognised. I'm a great believer in meditation. I don't mean six hours in the temple with orange robes and scented candles. No, but twenty minutes a day put aside for meditative contemplation can bring real rewards. It can help maximise performance, boost concentration and increase creativity. I meditate every day before I get on the hamster wheel, and then again during lunchtime. I find it gives my mind clarity, improves my focus and reduces stress. When you're juggling three businesses, two children, losing both your parents ten months apart in the middle of a global pandemic and trying to write a book, I can tell you the stress, pressure and responsibility would tip some people over the edge. Without meditation I wouldn't be coping. It's so important to allow your brain some downtime to switch off and recharge. It has a similar effect to regular exercise, but for the brain.

Recruitment life is hard. You need a healthy mental release from it, otherwise the long-term strain will take its toll and you'll end up either a burnt-out cautionary tale or a failed recruiter. Meditation can help you get your mind in the right place, putting you in the best position to succeed. There has been so much written on the subject that it won't take you long to find a guide or a local teacher, or even an app on your mobile phone. I had the privilege of meeting Bristol entrepreneur Andy Puddicombe. Andy is a trained Buddhist monk who co-founded the Headspace app to spread health and happiness by teaching us to slow down. It's become part of my life since then – a very positive activity that adds real value – like buying a gym membership for the mind!

'You should sit in meditation for 20 minutes a day, unless you are too busy, then you should sit for an hour.' – old Zen saying

---

Environmental Influences

In the Office

'You are the average of the five people you hang out with' is a well-known saying. In any competitive sport, the more you play with other people better than yourself, the more you improve. You also tend to up your game when the competition is harder. When we're up against our greatest competitors we try that little bit harder, don't we?

The same applies to recruitment and many other jobs. Behaviour breeds behaviour – if you surround yourself in the office with the people who are always making excuses, what will you learn except bad behaviour? *A fixed mindset.*

If you surround yourself with the most successful consultants: a) you'll learn from them, and b) you'll find you become more successful because you're learning the same values and sharing the same motivations. You're developing *a growth mindset*. Talk to your boss, hang out with the biggest biller. You'll find that people's natural inclination is actually to help other people. If we're successful, we like the acknowledgement that curiosity brings. Yes, we're all in our own little bubbles to some extent, but my door is always open and I will always give anyone my time and energy if they truly want it and will use it positively. When I first became successful in recruitment, I used to speak with my Managing Director every week – a quick catch-up about where I was going and how I was getting there. Failing consultants in the office tend to be the ones who go on smoking breaks together and moan together. They reinforce one another's bad habits and justify excuses.

Friends and Family

This may sound harsh, but values and aspirations differ and change over time. It's important to surround yourself with friends who have similar goals, values, desires and dreams to you. Over the past twenty years, there have been times when the people around me were not bringing out the best in me but were dragging me down instead. I decided to say goodbye to them. Not in a negative way, as you always want to be on good terms with everyone, but I just chose to spend my time with people who were more likely to help me achieve what I wanted to.

By cutting out the negative influencers from your life you're consciously walking a path that's more aligned with what you actually want and you're increasing your chances of getting it. Now, in my close friendship network, we help one another achieve our goals.

Take a moment just to pause and ask yourself, right now, who in your life is preventing you from achieving your goals? Who would support your dreams and encourage your success? Who challenges you to be the best version of yourself? In truth you cannot separate work and life influences, because one will surely impact on the other. Look at Maslow's hierarchy again.

Negativity is the worst thing you can expose yourself to. You want to be surrounded with people – in and out of the office – who are positive about what they do and how they do it. Not in an annoying way – just in a grown-up, competitive but empathetic manner. To paraphrase Will Smith in *The Pursuit of Happyness*, *'don't ever let anyone tell you can't do something'*. If people tell me I can't do something, that I'm not good enough, it feeds me – I thrive off that. In my workplace everyone is different – I certainly wouldn't want 25 replicas of me. The important thing is that we're all working towards similar goals and supporting each other in doing that. Remove or distance the mood hoovers and negative influencers from your life, even if you're related to them!

Distractions

Here are my important distractions, my 'Grade A, you can interrupt me and will get my undivided attention' distractions:

1. A member of my family is ill
2. The office is burning down
3. A client owes us money and is going under
4. A member of staff is leaving or something serious has happened to them
5. We're losing a client
6. We're losing a placement
7. A global catastrophe/ pandemic (maybe).

I can be barged in on at any time in any of these scenarios. Everything else can wait until I'm ready for it. If you're engaged in an exercise – for two or three hours – you need to be fully focused. So, grade your distractions into A, B and C categories.

A= important and urgent – it needs my attention now
B = important, but not urgent – beneficial, but not as important as what I am doing
C = it can wait.

There are distractions you can manage. You can turn off notifications from non-productive apps on your phone while you're at work, for instance. A phone pinging every five minutes will take you away from your task. Some distractions are less easy to deal with, but you need to anyway. Consider. If your boss interrupts your valuable work by asking you to do something, you need to manage upwards. Rather than saying *'No, I can't do it'*, reframe your response. Ask, *'How urgent is it? When do you need it by?*

Can I do it by this time?' If they are insistent, politely explain the urgency of what you are doing. No boss is going to want you to lose a placement or an interview to take the pressure off them for an hour or two.

If you're head-hunting for an important role and need to be fully cognisant of a candidate's responses, then shut off the environmental distractions of the office. Take yourself into a quiet room where you can concentrate 100 per cent on what you are asking and the replies you are getting. Master your distractions.

A good understanding of your motivations, mindset and environment is absolutely essential to help you achieve your ambitions in work and in life. Later, we're going to put that understanding into practice, by getting you to look more closely at your strengths and weaknesses, to set yourself some goals and ensure you can achieve them.

THE LIMITLESS RECRUITER WILL KNOW THAT...

- **What motivates you will determine the goals that you set for yourself – in your life and in your career**
- **To keep yourself motivated, you need rewards and recognition**
- **A growth mindset is the most important component of your training**
- **Your environment contributes to your performance in positive and negative ways**
- **There are welcome distractions, and important ones, and there are ones which are a complete waste of time**
- **You are the average of the five people you hang out with.**

Chapter Nine:
A Limitless Recruiter Masterclass

*'The definition of insanity is doing the same thing over and over
and expecting different results.' – Albert Einstein*

Part One: Goals and Goal-Setting
- Goal-Setting – the Recipe and Ingredients
- How to Analyse your Desk and Set the Right Key Performance Indicators
- Output / Input Measurables
- Using the Wheel of Life to Find your Goals
- Making your Goals SMART.

Part Two: Planning and Organisation
- Achieving Your Goals
- Time Management
- Milestones
- Breaking Goals Into Plans
- The Weekly Timetable
- When to Do Things and How to Prioritise
- The Day Planner
- Tips and Tricks to Achieve Your Goals.

THE ART OF RECRUITMENT

INTRODUCTION

The key to any success in recruitment is that you should always be learning and improving – it's the growth mindset we discussed in the last chapter. Only the arrogant believe they know it all. If you do the same things over and over again, are you going to improve? No. Sometimes you need to make changes. In order to upgrade your performance, if you truly want to become one of the great limitless recruiters, you have to have an understanding of what that performance is – where you match or exceed expectations, but also where you might be falling short. You need to step out of the hamster wheel and take a look at yourself; assess where you are and where you want to be; and then set yourself up for success. Sounds easy, doesn't it?

One area that always stands out as a key factor for success, not only in recruitment but in life, is goal-setting. Alastair Campbell (spin doctor, journalist and author of *Winners: And How They Succeed*) studied the world's greatest leaders, from athletes to politicians, film stars to entrepreneurs, to find out what all of them had in common that helped them achieve their ambitions, and what it took to succeed. Guess where it all starts? Having the right goals. It's also one of the six DNA strands that make a Limitless Recruiter. If you truly want to succeed in recruitment, it's vital that you have the right goals.

In this section I'm going to show you how to set the right goals, and how to organise your time and form a rock-solid plan in order to achieve them. I've also added some tips and tricks to help you along the way. To keep it simple, I've divided it into two parts.

PART ONE: GOALS AND GOAL SETTING

THE ART OF RECRUITMENT

---

*'Goal – the object of a person's ambition or effort;
an aim or desired result.'*

What goals *do* you have? It sounds like a basic question. Everyone has goals, surely? You'd be surprised at the number of people I've interviewed over the years – either as new recruiters or as candidates – who don't have any goals they want to achieve past the daily grind or monthly budget. Or they have a few ideas of what they'd like to achieve – at some point – but don't have any specifics, measurables or any idea of how to get there. Guess what? As a result, these people often achieve inconsistent results and, over time, become stale and frustrated in their career, feeling that they are going nowhere.

"Without goals, and plans to reach them, you are like a ship that has set sail with no destination." – Fitzhugh Dodson, American clinical psychologist, lecturer, and educator.

GOAL SETTING – THE RECIPE AND INGREDIENTS

The goals you set yourself need to motivate you, excite you and challenge you. They also need to be attainable. If you don't believe you can achieve them, then you'll quickly become disheartened. Think of goal-setting as being like cooking a delicious dinner: if you want to savour every mouthful and enjoy the rewards of your efforts, you must make sure you have the right ingredients and the right recipe.

Like a recipe, you'll want to break your goals down into easy-to-follow instructions, so that you can achieve one stage before moving onto the next. That way you won't be daunted by the targets you set yourself and the end goals will be more visible.

Try to make sure you have goals in each of the following areas – at all times. This will keep you busy, stimulated and focused. The variety will prevent you becoming stale and also give you a real sense of satisfaction and achievement – both in and out of the office.

A great tool to help you pinpoint your goals is the Wheel of Life, explained later on.

• *Financial* – as a minimum, your manager should give you a target for each month, quarter and year. These will vary depending on your agency's targets, the sector you work in and the role you have. But there's nothing to stop you setting your own goals in addition – maybe to achieve the biggest placement fee you can, or achieving a record month of £30k, for instance.

• *Business Development/Account Management* – try to think of goals in this category from as many angles as you can. What does your client base look like? Which are your top ten companies? Which one is the biggest spender? What clients would you like to work with who aren't currently on your list? Which client on your list offers the most potential for development over the next year? Which clients might be open to PSLs or exclusivity agreements? Is there a new sector or region you'd like to focus on and develop in the next twelve months?

• *Candidate Strategy* – how many placements do you want to make, and where will they come from? Which job vacancy do you want to fill time and time again, and what network activity will you need to achieve this? Is there a new role becoming more sought after – perhaps because of a change in market conditions? Should you switch to temp from perm – or consider doing both? Have you got a Top 20 list of candidates? How proactive are you being in identifying every potential candidate in your network? Should you consider taking on more senior roles with higher placement fees?

• *Personal Development* – What skills do you want to improve on? What's the biggest single area that would – with the right training and development – improve your ability to achieve? Break down your role, using the Wheel of Life (below).

Development is mental and physical, and environmental as well. Consider seeking mentors in and outside of work. *In work* – to help you improve your techniques in areas such as head-hunting, negotiating or interviewing. *Outside of work* – to advise you on factors like improving your knowledge of business, the sector and your mindset. One goal reinforces the other. Your mentors don't have to be people you know – you can sign up for online mentoring. There are so many options these days.

• *Career* – What's your next step? What then? Where next? What are the career milestones you foresee for yourself and what goals must you have to reach them?

• *Your Profile* – how can you increase your profile in a tough market-place? How can you utilise your company's resources and your networks to do this? Think of concrete goals you can set. Maybe boosting your LinkedIn profile with regular blogs.

Exploiting your black book of contacts to turn them into closer contacts. This is vital for any wannabe Limitless Recruiter. I set my each of my team a goal of becoming good friends with one or two of the best-connected affiliates in the industry. Why? Most people love work gossip and as a recruiter, clients will want to talk to you if you know what's happening in their industry. It will raise your profile and put you on their speed dial. They will take your calls, as you are the recruiter in the know! Remember, as my old MD used to say, *knowledge is power*. People want to know who's going under, who landed that contract, which senior member is leaving to join a competitor, or what the issue is in the supply chain.

One great way to gain credibility, and therefore business, is to get testimonials. After every successful placement, ask both the client and the candidate for a recommendation of your service. Make it visible for everyone to see on LinkedIn and other social media, and on your company website. You can even put the best ones on your email signature and include them on mailshots. People trust good reviews more than any other type of marketing, so use them. You've worked hard for the recommendations, so you should be proud of them and share them.

- *WIIFM ('What's In It For Me?!')* – what are you going to do with the fruits of your success? What are you going to spend the money on? A new electric car? A bigger house? You must have personal goals which spur you on to succeed in recruitment: these are really important as motivators. The second I rocked up to my desk at Hill McGlynn, I stuck an A4 picture of a black Porsche

911 turbo on the board, just like the one Will Smith was driving in the 1995 film, *Bad Boys*. I had dreamt about that car after first seeing that film at the age of thirteen and when I landed a role where I could actually get one off the back of my hard work, I made sure I knew exactly what I needed to do to succeed. By my thirtieth birthday that dream was a reality. Could I have got it sooner? Yeah, of course, but becoming a dad at twenty-two meant my personal goals changed. Having a house and putting my son through private education came first.

• *Feel Good Factor/ Contribution Goals* – what are the things – aside from the above factors – which are likely to give you real satisfaction and get you out of bed in the morning and staying late at the office to complete them? What puts a smile on your face? *Make them goals.*

For me, it's helping recruiters to improve, succeed and achieve their goals – that's why I'm writing this book. For other people, it could be supporting a favourite client, or contributing to the well-being of the sector they work in. What new venture could you start to push yourself above and beyond the call of duty? How about organising a big charity event to raise money (and your profile), which improves your fitness at the same time – win, win, win! Or working with a charity that helps get people back into work? We work with a variety of people at Kingston Barnes – ranging from ex-military to former offenders and the long-term unemployed – all looking for an opportunity to achieve their goals. These things matter. Getting fulfilment, as well as success, is a basic human need and nothing warms your soul better.

HOW TO ANALYSE YOUR DESK AND MAKE KEY PERFOR-
MANCE INDICATORS WORK FOR YOU

The first thing I ask any recruiter, whether they have 20 years' experience or 20 minutes', is – aside from money on the board – how do you measure your success in your role? The answers most recruiters give is 'Key Performance Indicators (KPIs)', and rightly so. Key Performance Indicators are the measure of activities and behaviours needed to achieve success in your role. They are the ingredients and the recipe to make your award-winning recruitment meal! So how can you improve these result areas, if you do not measure and analyse them?

KPIs get a bad rap in our industry. A lot of recruiters say they hate KPIs and recruitment companies will claim they don't have a KPI culture, and that's mainly because of how managers use this information – if they use it at all!

So let's get all the reasons why recruiters might hate KPIs out of the way:

1. They are unrealistic and unachievable.
2. The wrong KPIs have been set and they feel like a box-ticking exercise – rather than a positive contribution to a desired outcome.
3. There are too many KPIs to measure – it feels as though you're back at school.
4. I am an experienced recruiter now and don't need them anymore – KPIs are for trainees.
5. They are always the same. Nothing new or creative comes out of them to increase productivity.

> *'There are those who make things happen, those who watch*
> *things happen, and those who wonder what happened.'*
> *– John Newbern's Law.*

KPIs should never be set just for the sake of it. Any politician or manager can make stats, facts and figures work in their favour to prove a point. In recruitment, if KPIs are used correctly, they can be the difference between a blank month and a record-breaking month. A Limitless Recruiter will use them to help improve performance, month in, month out.

Once you begin to measure volumes of activity you will be able to spot efficiencies, meaning that you can avoid doing more work for less return! Measuring and improving efficiencies enables you to see how you can obtain improved results for the same effort – even better when you're working flat out, and can't physically do anymore, but still want to increase performance.

Put simply, the proper use of KPIs is a matter of being aware of what it is you need to do on a daily basis to succeed. Typically, recruiters underperform in the following areas:

With Clients
- Poor ratio of sales calls to obtaining vacancies
- Not knowing the best questions to ask during sales calls
- Taking a detailed vacancy and not qualifying everything
- Not enough proactive client meetings
- Low ratio of client exclusivity

- Poor client qualification – not understanding the difference between A, B and C clients
- Over-reliance on CVs – not closing clients to see the people they have recommended verbally
- Little to no focus on networking accounts and Strategic Account Management
- Not FAB selling (Features, Advantages, Benefits) when marketing candidates
- Not closing for commitment on a desired outcome, e.g. interview slots, exclusivity on next vacancies, etc.

With Candidates
- Not qualifying candidates effectively enough
- Not asking the right questions to uncover problems
- Low ratio of star candidate exclusivity
- Poor interview preparation for candidates
- Not enough new candidate generation
- Lack of alternative opportunities for candidates.

Their Desk
- Bad time management
- Lack of detailed and motivated goals and objectives
- Low interview to placement ratio
- Poor ratio of CVs sent to interviews arranged
- Not covering every Grade A vacancy with multiple candidates.

Whatever stage of your career you're at, when analysing your desk you need to know what you have to do to reach the desired outcome at each stage of the journey. So, how many sales calls do you need to make to get a vacancy? How many new vacancies do you obtain exclusively? How many CVs do you need to send to get an interview? How many interviews do you need to arrange to make a placement? What percentage of vacancies are not filled? One of my favourites – how many interviews arranged before sending a CV? Where are your vacancies coming from – is it one client or multiple clients?

And your candidates – where are you finding them, and how many new candidates do you register each week? Your placements made – are they all vacancy-led, speculative-led, or a combination of both?

If you start to pick apart all your activity and track the detail, you can see where the areas are for improvement in your performance – where the gaps are. When analysing your desk, you should be able to drill down into what's happening, what the key productivity indicators should be for the desired output you want, and then you can identify areas for improvement and set the right input goals to achieve them.

Output / Input Measurables

The first stage in goal-setting is to be aware of what a successful year for you would look like. You have to think of the *outputs* you want to achieve, and then calculate the necessary *inputs* for you to get there. So if you could only set yourself targets for three outputs which would make it an amazing year for you, what would they be? Most people, wisely, keep these outputs simple. Usually, at least one of these outputs will be financial – it'll be something like, *I want to bill £240,000 in a year.*

One of your output goals should be recruitment-related, with your financial goal firmly in mind. It might be record-led – getting your biggest number of placements, or your biggest quarter, for instance.

Make your third one something outward-looking – something client-led – so it might be that you want to bill £100,000 with a single client, or turn over £1 million with three clients.

With these output goals in mind, you can start to break them down, which will make it easier to grasp the idea of the necessary inputs you'll have to make to achieve them.

So, taking the output goal above of billing £240k in a year, that means you will need to bill an average of £60k a quarter, or £20k a month. By breaking it down like this you can see the milestones you have to be hitting.

Sticking with that goal, how many placements do you need to achieve £20k a month? What's your average placement fee? How many vacancies do you need to generate the interviews to make those placements? Look at your past performance figures and also consider where you might improve your performance to make these targets more attainable. For instance, if your interview to placement ratio is lower than other consultants in your office, you might want to set yourself a goal of improving that – by analysing what happened after each interview. Why didn't it progress? Was it a lack of preparation with the candidate? Was the match not quite right? Were salary expectations way off, or did the candidate have two better offers?

The effective analysing and planning of your inputs, with these factors in mind, is key to achieving your outputs. And this goes further than how you plan your quarterly performance. In truth, you won't become a Limitless Recruiter without properly planning your weeks and your days.

THE WHEEL OF LIFE

This tool has been invaluable to me over the years. I've adapted it from several similar models I've come across in life coaching situations. It's a simple method that allows you, at a glance, to visualise your strengths and areas for improvement. If you're struggling to identify where to prioritise your efforts – either in the office or in your personal development – then I guarantee that this will help you see the wood for the trees.

Draw a circle and then divide it into ten segments, with lines from the centre of the circle to the perimeter. Now draw a circle halfway between the perimeter and the centre. Label the centre with a 'zero' and the point where each line meets the perimeter with a '10.'

You should have – either on paper or on your computer – an illustration that looks a little bit like a dartboard. The Wheel here has been filled in with categories I used for my team at Kingston Barnes, but you can adapt it to suit your needs.

This simple tool has become the foundation of all the personal development planning and goal-setting that I do. I draw a Wheel of Life regularly to check that I'm where I want to be and not falling behind in the areas where I've identified that my performance needs improving, and I'm suggesting that you do exactly this now.

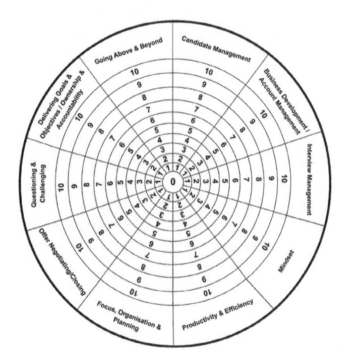

You can use it solely to gauge your recruitment performance or, as I do, to gauge personal goals as well, which – since you're reading this book – should still, of course, include becoming a Limitless Recruiter.

So in a recruitment context, considered in more detail below, you'll need to label each segment with the ten key areas which make up your job description. Similarly – for personal goals – you might include headings like Money and Finances, Health and Fitness, Romance, Family and Friends, Fun, Personal Development, Your Environment and, of course, your Career.

The beauty of the Wheel of Life is that it allows you to see clearly, in an instant, where you are at – areas where you're meeting your expectations and areas where you're falling short and need to improve. This is a great way to pinpoint where to focus your attention and decide on your goals – both in and out of the office.

The Wheel of Life for Recruitment

The Wheel of Life is designed to raise your awareness of your abilities and of the areas of your performance which need improvement, so that you can equip yourself with the skills and knowledge necessary to be an expert in what you do.

Recruitment is like a conveyor belt. In order for you to end up with a constant run of placements, every part of the process needs to work seamlessly. If one of those areas isn't performing as well as the others, it'll lead to a halt in the production line and that's when a gap in your placements will occur. The Wheel will help you clarify priorities for goal-setting, which we're coming to next.

You're aiming for a balance of achievement and activity in all the areas that make up your role. Balance can be achieved over time and as your skills improve in some areas, you'll need to play catch-up in others. So label each segment of the Wheel with the categories which make up your position. These will most likely include the ubiquitous ones like Candidate Management, Business

Development, Client and Account Management, Interview Management, Client Meetings, Offer Negotiation / Converting. Everyone has slightly different job specifications, depending on their role, so just summarise the areas of every part of your job as best you can.

This should give you seven or eight categories. Then add a couple more, using the 'DNA of a Limitless Recruiter' chapter for inspiration – so perhaps Mindset and Work Ethic. You should now have ten segments.

Now you need to give yourself a score in each segment out of 10. Is your Candidate Management an '8'? Colour or shade in the segment to that point. Are your Client Meetings near perfection? Give that a '9'. Is your Business Development almost non-existent because you're devoting your energies elsewhere? Mark a '3' across the relevant segment. You'll probably end up – if you're being honest with yourself – with a circle showing a pretty uneven line running around it. (I hardly need to say that there's no point in filling it in if you're not prepared to be honest with yourself. It often helps to get a second opinion, too – from a trusted work colleague or friend.) To achieve true balance on a path of continuous development and success, imagine it like a wheel. If a wheel isn't even and round it won't move forward, will it? No, and neither will you. Plotting your Recruitment Wheel every three to six months can highlight where you've upgraded and where you've got left behind.

You can also plot other Wheels to go into more detail in one area. Say you've given Client and Account Management a '1'. Break it down into ten further sections, on a separate Wheel, to figure out what you need to improve on – like identifying key decision-makers, objection handling, promoting you or the company you represent, taking a detailed vacancy, presenting CVs, maximising key accounts and networking.

Now, looking at the Recruitment Wheel, here are some great questions to ask yourself to take the exercise deeper:

- Are there any surprises for you?
- How do you feel about your skills as you look at your Wheel?
- How do you currently spend time in these areas? How would you like to spend time in these areas?
- What would make a score of 10 in each segment?
- Which of these categories would you most like to improve?
- What could you do to change your scores positively in these categories by, say, one or two points?
- What help and support might you need to improve?
- What change should you make first? And what change do you want to make first?
- If there was one key action you could take that would begin to bring everything into balance, what would it be?
- What would prevent you from being able to achieve these changes?

Taking action – the final step. To wrap up this exercise, identify the improvements needed for each segment of the Wheel, goals that you want to develop, and then make a note of them. You might have multiple goals for each segment, or just one in some cases.

There's always room for improvement in everything we do, so think carefully and use the KPIs above to help you identify what will help you the most, moving forward.

The key take-away is that you're making forward momentum and you now have the right goals to lead you down the right path – the yellow brick road, you might call it – towards the wonderful land of Limitless Recruitment.

The Limitless Recruiter will look at the Wheel of Life and:

• Ask, *What is the smallest step I could take to get started?*
• Consider, *What little things could I do to take a segment up by one mark? What big things could I do to jump it up by two or three?*
• Realise that taking action may mean doing some things differently – pushing yourself out of your comfort zone, making new routines. Don't be afraid to embrace the new!
• Acknowledge that it takes 30 days to make a habit, 90 days to make a lifestyle. Persistence and practice are the keys.
• In each segment ask, *What would be total fulfilment for me? What is my 10?* That's your starting point, your goal.

SETTING SMART GOALS

When you're working out your goals, you need to make sure that they're SMART:

THE ART OF RECRUITMENT

'Whatever your walk in life, it's only when you are SMART
(Specific, Measurable, Attainable, Relevant and Time-limited)
about your objective that you can begin to design and implement
a clear strategy to meet it.' – Alastair Campbell, spin doctor and
author of 'Winners: And How They Succeed'.

Specific and Measurable

You have to be focused in your goals. An objective like 'be a better recruiter' is too vague because how will you know that you're doing the *specific* things which will enable you to improve, and how will you be able to *measure* whether that improvement has occurred because of your goal setting, rather than just by chance?

In practice this means it's not enough to just say *'I want to...'*: you must work out how to make it happen – and by when. Taking the time to break the goals into smaller steps makes them feel less daunting and more achievable. This will help keep you motivated and on track. And what if the steps you identify push your goal back? That's just fine. The single most important thing is to work out a realistic road map of how you're going to make it happen – and stick to it.

Attainable

Nothing will set you up to fail more than over-reaching. Everybody loves an optimist and ambition is key – but keep it real. With the best will in the world, it's unlikely that even the most promising recruitment researcher will make the transition to senior consultant in three months. Instead of trying to conquer the whole world in a single leap, it's far more productive to break that journey down into stages that you know you can pick off within a realistic time frame. But equally, don't aim for average either. It's important you push yourself past your limitations, or you will never know what you are truly capable of. I left a senior director's position with a six-figure salary, which I could quite comfortably have remained in until now. Instead, I followed my dreams and now have a company ten times the size of my former agency that's won countless awards, turns over millions of pounds and has helped place thousands (yes, thousands) of people into new jobs. *#worthit*

Part of making sure your goals are attainable is to know what has been achieved in your role – not just by you, but in the office. You'll need to be familiar with what is considered successful and achievable before you can set your own goals. Whilst it sounds good, there's probably little point in setting yourself a billing target of £1 million in an office where the average consultant is billing £60k a year unless you know something they don't – if a blue chip corporation is moving into your region and you're best friends with the board of Directors – in which case, fill your boots!

Relevant

Talk to friends, colleagues or managers about your objectives, to make sure they're the right ones to keep you on track. Don't be afraid to reach out to someone in a leadership position in your field and ask for five minutes of their time. You might be surprised how one single piece of feedback or advice can trigger an avalanche of inspiration.

People who have already successfully trodden the path you want to follow can be not only a great inspiration but also a fantastic source of information. They know what you need to do to get from A to B. Building relationships with your successful colleagues is a great way to help you move up the career ladder more quickly and perform better. Fact.

Time-limited

The only time to hit a target is when you can see it. Create a twelve-month career timeline and keep it somewhere visible. Now it's down to you to keep an eye on that countdown and tick off every milestone and objective along the way. Imposing more deadlines in a role already full of them may seem like introducing additional stress, but it's a great way to keep you focused on your progress and you'll be able to see it, too. Having time-limited objectives gives you something to get up for in the morning – mapping your progress by ticking off milestones to that goal will give you a sense of achievement and purpose.

PART TWO:

PLANNING AND ORGANISATION

THE ART OF RECRUITMENT

ACHIEVING YOUR GOALS

So, now you have your SMART goals, what to do you need to do to achieve them? You obviously need the processes described in the second part of this book, but good planning and organisation are also vital.

The great thing about recruitment is that it's actually really simple to break it down. It's time to make those goals more manageable. You do this by working out what milestones you'll need to reach on the journey to your goal.

Let's recap the simple financial target we discussed earlier – billing £240,000 over the next twelve months. Break it down. How much will you need to bill over the next six months? £120,000. The next three months? £60,000. The next month? £20,000.

Now look at the goal from a recruitment perspective. How many people would you need to place to get that result? If your average fee is £5,000, you'll need to make fifty placements over the year, or just over four placements a month. So straightaway you know how many placements you'll need to make every month, on average, to achieve your goal. This will be one of your milestones.

From this, you can start to plan the process. How many interviews will you need to make to attain five placements a month? The rule of average is that roughly one out of four interviews – if properly arranged – should lead to a placement. So, you'll need to arrange 20 interviews per month.

How many vacancies will you need to take to make that interview target? And so on.

It doesn't matter what level of recruitment you're working at, or in what field. You could be Senior Executive Search Consultant, a Temporary Driving Recruiter or an Account Manager specialising in placing IT professionals – the three basics common to all are placements, vacancies and interviews. You need to be securing all three on a regular basis to keep the wheel turning smoothly. The key to being a Limitless Recruiter is knowing how many of each you need to achieve the outcome you want. You do this by looking at past results and projecting what you can achieve if you raise your game in each of these areas. You then need to plan and organise your time to your maximum benefit.

TIME MANAGEMENT

To become a Limitless Recruiter – someone who's billing £500k and decides they want to bill, say, £1 million instead – you're going to need to think very carefully about how you manage your time. What are you doing with your time, and what results are you getting from it? If you work a 50-hour week, what exactly are you doing with those 50 hours?

What does your week look like at the moment? What does a typical day look like?

What are the key things that you're doing? A good recruiter should be working on about twenty activities every week. If you had to break down your activities and put a pound sign against each one – which of your activities contribute the most to your success?

But time management is also thinking about 'when'. For instance, if you want to make twenty interviews by the end of the week then you'll probably want to make sure you get your CVs out nice and early in the week – on Monday or Tuesday. If you wait until Thursday or Friday, it may be too late.

Basically, when considering your productivity you need to think what's the highest chance of success, and what's the easiest route to get there? A lot of people place much more emphasis on the input than the output, but output is the most important measure. You simply need to work back from the output to work out what you need to do to achieve it.

At Kingston Barnes we obtain a really high percentage of our placements from head-hunting, so we spend more time and energy on that activity than the average agency probably does. Every agency, region and sector will have strengths and weaknesses – make sure you're playing to the strengths in your situation.

MILESTONES

When you're confronted with the set of goals you've set yourself for the next quarter or twelve months, it may seem a little overwhelming. Just as, if you said to yourself, *'I'm going to drive to Moscow next week,'* you might start to panic. Don't worry. You're going to break this down into manageable tasks.

Once you have an idea of where you want to get to, goal-setting is like getting from A to Z in a car. The first thing you need is transportation – your motivation and mindset. The second is the destination – your goals. Finally, your plan is the map or strategy you use for getting you there.

Back to my car and destination analogy. It's a long journey

you're about to embark on. As well as the objectives and the map to get you there, you'll need some milestones along the route because you'll need signs that you're still going in the right direction and at the right speed.

So if you have a list of goals over twelve months, for example, mark when you expect to attain each goal. These will be your milestones. Keep referring to this list as you progress and mark and reward yourself when you achieve each individual milestone on your journey. If a goal is proving more difficult than you anticipated, you may need to revise it at the relevant point – one month, three months, six months or twelve months. That's OK – in fact it shows you are in control of the process, which is the key to becoming a Limitless Recruiter.

You may have decided that your knowledge about your sector might be inadequate, for instance. So, what will your task be? *I'm going to do a presentation to myself or my team on the sector and the key roles within it.* By when? *I'm going to give myself two weeks to do it.* Stick it in as one of your three goals for the first month. Or you might decide to make a list of the top 100 key companies within that sector, find out who their key decision-makers are and try to meet them all within six months. It's up to you. Well, it's up to you but you will probably want to let your boss know that this is your goal. In fact, let everyone know. Another secret to success with any goal is to share your ambitions with people you trust. They will spur you on to succeed and, if you fail to reach a goal, help you understand why. Remember to *learn, learn, learn* from any unachieved goal – it's the growth mindset.

THE ART OF RECRUITMENT

'What is the task? What is the action? By when?'

BREAKING GOALS INTO PLANS

Annual goals are good and necessary, but try and break them down into 90-day – quarterly – chunks. That way you can adjust your course, if you need to, but you'll also get a sense of achievement at regular intervals, rather than fretting about whether you're going to achieve the Big One.

Working to more than a 90-day plan can lead to procrastination, because you don't feel the urgency when something is so far in the distance. Believe me, I've seen it happen time and time again. What you need is a short-term approach to your long-term goals.

Each quarter, you should be sitting down to review your performance. If this isn't company policy at your agency, do it for yourself anyway. Look at the revenue targets you set yourself for these three months and compare them with your actual performance. It's also a perfect time, and a decent period, to review your KPIs. With more data you'll be able to notice patterns and see room for improvement. Areas where you can maximise success – what you aren't doing, and why. And areas where you are wasting your time.

Check the objectives you set yourself at the end of the last quarter and see how you measured up to them – where you excelled and where you fell down. Use your analysis to plot the next three months. Pick out the areas on the Wheel of Life where you could improve and set yourself targets which will help you get there.

Break down the necessary activities into weeks so that you can keep a close eye on the progress you're making.

THE WEEKLY TIMETABLE

Remember back at school when you were given your weekly timetable? You knew exactly what classes you'd be attending, on which day, and for how long. How often did you miss a lesson? Not often, I bet, unless it was deliberate and you were skiving off! There is a reason it was scheduled that way. Imagine if you did this with every task and every goal – allocated the right amount of time for each task, week in, week out. In theory, there shouldn't be a reason why you wouldn't get everything done that you wanted to, is there?

Without wishing to give you nightmares about returning to the classroom, if you don't map out the week ahead and know exactly what you are going to do and when, guess what will happen? It won't get done: not all of it, anyway.

How many times have I had a consultant, at the end of a week, giving me excuses as to why they haven't achieved four out of five objectives they set themselves the previous week? – *'I haven't had the time; I've been too busy; the dog ate my plan...'*

The goals you set yourself on a weekly basis are there for a reason. If you're not achieving them, you're not planning your week right. A Limitless Recruiter will always over-achieve their objectives. That, in a nutshell, is what success is – the ability to over-achieve targets, week in, week out. If they're too busy – and this does happen – then they'll delegate. It's called Time Management.

So how do you plan the week ahead? How do you prioritise your activities for each day? You need to use the Urgent/Important method, outlined below.

WHEN TO DO THINGS AND HOW TO PRIORITISE
You've got to allocate the right time to the right priorities. So, write down the twenty things you're going to do in the following week and then grade them – A, B, C or D – according to the following useful scale:

A – Important and Urgent
These are tasks which must be tackled now – emergencies, deadlines and scheduled appointments. In recruitment terms, these would include vacancies with important clients which need filling urgently and a client visit to a new company with great potential. Deal with these straight away – no ifs, no buts!

B – Important but Not Urgent
Actually more important than tasks in category 'A' – these are the activities which will help you achieve your goals. The things you've got to plan to do as soon as possible. Specific projects, new candidate generation and business development fall into this category. You need to be doing these things every day and planning more for future days.

C – Urgent but Not Important
These are the time-absorbent activities which are often best ignored

or delegated to others. They include writing new job adverts, or returning a call to a candidate chasing you for a response who's just sent you their CV and applied for a position they're not qualified for anyway. Try to get someone to do these tasks for you – if you can.

D – Not Urgent and Not Important
Everything else – the distractions you allow to deflect your attention from 'B' and 'A' activities. A list of them might include responding to a random LinkedIn message from an old work colleague, re-arranging your desk and shredding all the old CVs you've stacked up, or trialling a new bit of recruitment software that you don't really need. Anything that allows you to procrastinate and avoid getting down to the work you need to do in order to achieve your goals and become a Limitless Recruiter. The best bit of advice I can give you is to delete this list. Or have a shit list / folder and put everything in there. If and when something on it becomes important and urgent enough it can come out of the box. Until then, keep these distractions away from yourself.

THE DAY PLANNER
Every single day, 80 per cent of what I do is tasks that I know need to be done that day – the 'A' tasks. This helps me to create the activity I need to achieve the output I want from that day, so the other 20 per cent can be used to do things which are important but not so urgent – 'B' activities, like business development with an existing client when you have enough Grade A vacancies to work on. You may need to concentrate on filling live vacancies today,

but you need to know that there will be other vacancies coming down the line or else you're going to have a gap in the production line. So it's important that these activities are in the plan and get done at some point.

Divide your eight-hour day into two-hour chunks. Pick the six hours when you are most productive. These are the hours (the 80 per cent or so) when you're going to do your 'A' grade activity – your important and urgent tasks. Label them 1–10 in order of priority and just get through them as efficiently as you can. Tick them off the list and ignore any outside influences. A problem for many recruiters is that they have good intentions, but they never deliver because they're disorganised, or they get distracted and pulled into doing another activity.

Some people tend to be more productive at certain times of the day. For instance, if you only really feel alive after lunch, you might want to schedule your most important meetings in the afternoon and get on with your pressing admin in the morning. Or you may prefer working in the evening – it's often a good time to catch candidates who are otherwise busy themselves.

Use the other two hours of each day to get through the other 20 per cent of tasks – the 'important but not urgent,' and 'urgent but not important' jobs – delegating or ignoring as many as you can of the latter.

It's worth spending fifteen or twenty minutes at the end of your day to prepare and prioritise your workload for the next day. It takes a lot of the stress away if you just look at your list when you get in the office and think, *Right, that needs to be done by 9 am, that by midday, and those by mid-afternoon.* You can just sit down and get straight into it. And have regular pitstops during the day to check that you're where you need to be at that point.

I'd strongly recommend not spending longer than three hours on any one exercise. It gets repetitive and you lose your edge. Plus, spending too much time on any one activity increases your exposure to something going wrong. As an extreme example, I had a colleague who took ten vacancies from a favoured client. He thought, *'Brilliant, this is going to take up my whole week'.* He interviewed candidates and got twenty CVs over to the client by Friday afternoon, feeling really pleased with himself. On Monday, the client pulled all the jobs because of a financial crisis. So, my colleague's week had been a largely wasted effort.

You can keep your focus and your energy up by varying your routine – plan your day with this in mind. An old colleague of mine had a great tip, which I have found really helpful. Everyone has that one thing they don't want to do, have put off and are not looking forward to – do it first thing in the morning if you can. Get it out of the way because then nothing else you do will seem like such a chore, and it won't be hanging over you like a bad smell all day. Things like telling a candidate that they didn't get the job, or telling a client the candidate has rejected their offer and won't be turning up today – get them out of the way and then move on. Oh, and tell the client that you have someone else who is worth seeing and who can start immediately!

TIPS AND TRICKS TO ACHIEVE YOUR GOALS

We're all human and that means we're all vulnerable to bad days where concentration is lacking, or we're distracted by issues which can be trivial or important. There's no point pretending that we're going to turn in a perfect performance, hour after hour, day after day, week after week. But there are things we can do – habits we can form – which will enable us to perform to the best of our ability for the maximum amount of time. Here are some tips and tricks for helping you do just that.

Feedback

The most valuable information about your goal-setting and achievements should come from the person you already report to. Your boss can tell you your strengths and weaknesses, as well as areas for improvement. Take any negative comments on the chin and address any issues with an eye to the future. Constructive criticism is essential to everyone's self-development, so always use it to your advantage.

Effort

Nothing that was ever truly worthwhile is easy – and that's never been truer than with the future of your success in recruitment. There are no shortcuts when it comes to success — and proving that you're willing to put in the work is vital. People always notice hard work and that's one of the key ingredients to success. Effort, attitude and results.

Positivity

It's easy to become dispirited when all the pieces don't fall into place first time. But sometimes it really isn't you. The key is to stay motivated and inspired. You have a vision for your career, so just keep working away to make it happen. Believe in yourself and what you're capable of. Criticism can knock you off course, but sometimes it can inspire. Like many things in life, it's all about how you choose to look at it.

Effectiveness

You could have the most effective strategy in the world for career progress, but it won't do you any good if you don't measure your progress against your road map. Keep an eye on your milestone markers; don't beat yourself up if you miss them, but regroup, rethink and come back stronger to catch up.

Productivity and Efficiency

Being productive entails self-discipline and controlling your environment. How do you start your typical workday? If you're anything like most people, you probably check your inbox. As it turns out, this is a big mistake, because most emails are time wasters. So what should you do instead? As you've learned, being productive means doing as much as possible in as little time as possible, and only tackling projects that are important – that is, projects that bring you closer to your personal goals.

THE ART OF RECRUITMENT

The way to narrow things down is to weigh the importance of each activity by asking yourself, *'Would I be happy if this task ends up being the only one I complete today?'*

And if so, of course, because they're so important, these tasks should get top priority: you should turn to them first thing every morning, without even glancing at your emails. In an ideal workday, all the important tasks should be finished before midday.

A good way to start weaning yourself off minute-by-minute emails is to read and answer messages twice a day – once in the afternoon and once in the evening. Genuinely urgent requests can always be conveyed on the phone or in a face-to-face conversation. If it's that important, you'll soon know about it.

Also, keep in mind that spending a lot of time at work doesn't necessarily mean that you are addressing the right tasks, or that you are doing them well. Often the reverse is true. As Parkinson's Law* teaches us, the more time we have to complete a task, the more time we'll spend on it. So, if we have an hour to write up three CVs, profiles and references, we'll finish them in an hour. If we have the entire afternoon, it will take us four hours.

Similarly, the Pareto principle comes from an observation by Italian economist Vilfredo Pareto, that roughly 80 per cent of your results come from only 20 per cent of your efforts. Sounds about right, doesn't it? One thing I've learned is to prioritize those high-yielding 20 per cent of tasks and complete them in as little time as possible. This maximises productivity, reduces useless activity and, more often than not, increases revenue to boot. And we all like increased revenues, don't we?

[*Parkinson's Law is the old observation that work expands to fill the time available. The term was invented by Cyril Northcote Parkinson in an essay first published in 1955. Some things never change!]

One Final Tip

Aim big. There's less competition at the top. Don't just set yourself easy goals which you know can be obtained without much effort or improvement. That's not how you become a Limitless Recruiter!

THE LIMITLESS RECRUITER WILL...

- **Set attainable goals which are motivating, exciting and challenging**
- **Use Key Performance Indicators to help them determine what they need to do on a daily basis to succeed**
- **Use the Wheel of Life to raise awareness of their abilities and of the performance areas which need improvement, so that they can equip themselves with the skills and knowledge necessary to be an expert**
- **Set themselves SMART goals to keep themselves on target and on track**
- **Plan and organise their time to their maximum benefit.**

Chapter Ten: Lessons from Recruiting in a Pandemic

On the Friday before things got serious, our team was out celebrating at the Cheltenham Gold Cup. I'm not a gambling man, but I do love a day at the races, especially when I came away with a £5,000 winner! I thought my luck was in.

Ten days later, on Monday 23 March 2020, a national lockdown was announced and we were ordered to work from home. My agency went from having hundreds of thousands of pounds in the pipeline to nothing – all the horses had well and truly bolted in the opposite direction! We had placements told to stay put, hundreds of temporary workers sent home and multiple interviews at final stage cancelled. We had an immediately-available, director-level candidate negotiating a six-figure job offer due to start imminently, with a £30,000 fee banked in April. The client phoned to say they would have to postpone the offer until further notice. Every permanent and temporary vacancy had frozen, and all placements dried up.

Here was Lesson One: how you react to a crisis is vital.

Some agencies immediately made their staff redundant. On the news there were stories of panic buying – shortages of loo rolls, pasta and flour – as the virus spread. Lesson Two: avoid decisions based on emotion. It's good advice, but not easy to follow in an unprecedented situation such as this one. I normally follow a five-year plan, but that was ripped up. My agency's business plan? Ripped up. Month to month, quarter to quarter, year to year – none of it made any sense now. Instead, I was worried about how to keep the lights on and how to keep paying my team – the best team I'd ever had. My first priority was obviously to look after my children, wife and family. Next priority: business survival.

I had a chat with my senior management team. We had a certain amount of money stashed in the bank and decided we should batten down the hatches, sit tight and wait it out.

I told my recruitment team,

'We've got a nest egg that will last us for some time. Now, I'm not going to wind it down to zero and see all my savings from a twenty-year career disappear. However, we don't want to let you down either. You've given us total commitment since you joined us and in return, we will look after you as best we can for as long as we can.'

Nevertheless, our wage bill at that time was close to £100k a month, so there was a limit as to how generous we could be. Thankfully furlough kicked in soon after, vindicating our decision not to act too rashly.

Lesson Three: change your mindset. It was a real change of direction, requiring a change in thinking. We'd never had people working from home before. It seemed to go against everything that recruitment was about – meeting people, building relationships, seeing a client's working environment, and the all-important team banter and camaraderie in our office – which was the essence of why people loved working here in the first place.

Remote working meant ditching all this in favour of everyone going into their own little cells – be it the kitchen table, a corner of the living room or even the bedroom. The practicalities were mind-blowing enough. We had to shift phones and computers, get them up and running, and connected through a new cloud-based server to link everyone up.

Lesson Four: if there are no rules, you must make your own. There was no rulebook for the pandemic and no one had ever worked through a situation like it. Our vacancy list went from five hundred to five in a matter of days. Construction and manufacturing staff were at least classified as key workers, so some semblance of an industry continued once the pandemonium settled. It turned out that some clients did still need to hire – those in logistics, supermarkets, driving and engineering, in particular. This kept us going, but only about 10 per cent of the normal construction workforce was out there working.

Lesson Five: accept the reality. We accepted the new conditions and started looking for the opportunities because, as a Limitless Recruiter, I knew that there are always opportunities. It was the same with the global financial crash of 2007–2008 – you just had to know where to look.

So, what could we do? There were loads of candidates and no vacancies. For the first three months, no one was rebuilding. Everybody was holding their breath and closing their doors, waiting to see what would give. We had to hit the pause button. It was an opportunity to do all the non-urgent, non-important stuff that we'd been putting off. We rang all the companies that had vacancies with us. We were keeping the channels open – maintaining contact with clients on a weekly basis.

Lesson Six: decide what you can and can't control. These were uncharted waters –and things being out of my control was alien to me. I got into recruitment because I knew I could control every aspect of my performance. But now I needed to decide what it was in my power to influence and concentrate on that. Example: people were stuck at home – they could talk more freely now than when they were in the office. Head-hunting just got easier!

Lesson Seven: look at where the opportunities are. There are always opportunities. We concentrated on candidates. We contacted all the best candidates we could find and persuaded them that one day, this would end and there would be companies looking for the best people – urgently – to help them recover and 'build back better', as Boris would have it. We got them signed up to exclusivity deals. By the end of the first lockdown, we were primed and ready to go with candidates: their CVs were honed, our shelves were stacked! People who wanted to move, for whatever reason, were willing to be more flexible – because of the pandemic. All interviews had to be done online. *OK,* we decided*, We'll embrace it, rather than bemoaning our inability to meet candidates face-to-face.* We had our first offer from a Zoom interview three days after we had started using it.

Back in the virtual office, the team worked together on reduced hours. We were doing everything we could to keep the lights on, but keeping morale high was just as important. There were scared people. Mental health had never really been much discussed in recruitment – *work hard, play hard* was about the limit of it – but it became an issue during the pandemic. So in the summer of 2020 we went back to the races, this time online. We arranged for the whole team to receive food and wine packages, delivered to their homes, and had a great day betting on The Kingston Barnes Cup. We had wind-down Wednesdays, complete with quizzes and games like 'Through the Keyhole' and 'Countdown' – all over Zoom, of course. We had catch-ups and huddles and breakout meetings. The team learned a new way of working.

Lesson Eight: embrace change. Avoid a fixed mindset – everything is fluid. We began to see that this home working had potential benefits – and was not necessarily just a poor relation of office working. As a result, we've now adopted a flexible working policy. Everyone has two or three days at home and a couple of days in the office, each week. It works.

At the end of the second lockdown – at the start of 2021 – we saw huge investment and growth in the current market. It was like when Labour was elected in 1997 – enormous resources were committed to building back up. Now there were loads of vacancies but no candidates! We had to change strategy quickly. We had to increase all the activity towards the passive candidate market and lock down all active candidates. We told them a lesson we learned from the property market. If you have a house for sale with one board outside – people want to look. They're curious. If it has 20 boards outside – people are not so keen, and will never offer market value if someone seems desperate. *It's the same with candidates*, we said. We told them, *Take your details off the job boards and give us two weeks*. For the ones who trusted us and did this, we worked our socks off and put multiple offers on the table.

Lesson Nine: you must follow through on a promise. Do it.

The result was more candidates, more interviews per candidate and more job offers. We broke records for placements and fees three months in a row. One of our consultants filled thirteen permanent vacancies in a month, with an average fee of £6k. We're projecting growth of 25–50 per cent over the next five years and we're in the process of buying our own four-storey commercial premises in the most prestigious area of Bristol.

The grimmest time for me personally was the first month of lockdown. My dad was ill in hospital and sadly never recovered. I thought I was going to have to shut down the business that I'd worked so hard to set up and succeed with. I was having sleepless nights. Again, I thought about what I could control in this situation and what I couldn't. Mindset – if you receive bad news, what do you do? How do you react? I could control how I used my time, so I did. I learned to play chess to a good – not great – standard. I'm still working on that. I exercised daily and got really fit – fitter than I'd ever been in 20 years. I learned more about my dad in those last months than I had in the past five years. I spend hours with my sons every day – that was an opportunity the pandemic gave me which I never would have had otherwise.

I can truthfully say that we're a better company than we were before this crisis. And while it has been a stressful, difficult time, I have learned a lot from the challenges it has presented me with – both on a personal and on a business level. The pandemic just proved to me that the principles of Limitless Recruiting I have set out in this book work in any situation. Lesson Ten: trust the process!